1st EDITION

Perspectives on Diseases and Disorders

Malaria

Nancy Dziedzic
Book Editor

GALE
CENGAGE Learning™

Detroit • New York • San Francisco • New Haven, Conn • Waterville, Maine • London

Christine Nasso, *Publisher*
Elizabeth Des Chenes, *Managing Editor*

© 2010 Greenhaven Press, a part of Gale, Cengage Learning

Gale and Greenhaven Press are registered trademarks used herein under license.

For more information, contact:
Greenhaven Press
27500 Drake Rd.
Farmington Hills, MI 48331-3535
Or you can visit our Internet site at gale.cengage.com

For product information and technology assistance, contact us at

Gale Customer Support, 1-800-877-4253
For permission to use material from this text or product, submit all requests online at
www.cengage.com/permissions

Further permissions questions can be e-mailed to permissionrequest@cengage.com

Articles in Greenhaven Press anthologies are often edited for length to meet page requirements. In addition, original titles of these works are changed to clearly present the main thesis and to explicitly indicate the author's opinion. Every effort is made to ensure that Greenhaven Press accurately reflects the original intent of the authors. Every effort has been made to trace the owners of copyrighted material.

Cover image copyright Tom Stoddart/Hulton Archive/Getty Images.

LIBRARY OF CONGRESS CATALOGING-IN-PUBLICATION DATA

Malaria / Nancy Dziedzic, book editor.
   p. cm. -- (Perspectives on diseases and disorders)
 Includes bibliographical references and index.
 ISBN 978-0-7377-4379-1 (hardcover)
 1. Malaria. I. Dziedzic, Nancy G.
 RC156.M37 2009
 616.9'362--dc22

                                  2009026338

Printed in the United States of America
1 2 3 4 5 6 7 13 12 11 10 09

CONTENTS

Foreword   8

Introduction   10

CHAPTER 1   Understanding Malaria

1. An Overview of Malaria   16

Carol A. Turkington and Rebecca J. Frey

Malaria is a potentially deadly disease spread by infected mosquitoes and is endemic to certain countries in tropical regions, but it has in the past posed serious health threats in North America and Europe.

2. Malaria Is One of the Oldest and Deadliest Known Diseases   26

Michael Finkel

Despite global eradication efforts, malaria strikes more people now than ever before, with prevention, treatment, and the possibility of a vaccine at best imperfect solutions to the disease.

3. Pregnant Women Are the Adult Group Most Vulnerable to Malaria   36

Women Deliver

With lowered immunity to malaria, pregnant women are more likely to contract the disease, and women's overall low socioeconomic status in malaria-endemic countries means they are less able to access prevention methods and treatment and are therefore more vulnerable to malaria.

4. A Malaria Vaccine Shows Promise 42

Jean Stéphenne

A malaria vaccine developed and tested by the pharmaceutical company GlaxoSmithKline during 2008 has shown promise in preventing 53 percent of malaria episodes in children aged five to seventeen months.

CHAPTER 2 Controversies Surrounding Malaria Prevention and Treatment

1. African Countries Must Have Access to DDT to Eradicate Malaria 48

Sam Zaramba

A continued attitude of colonialism by Western countries toward African independence in disallowing the use of DDT in the fight against malaria is causing the unnecessary deaths of millions of Africans.

2. DDT Was Never Successful in Eradicating Malaria 54

Sonia Shah

The argument that malaria-endemic countries must have access to DDT to end the threat of malaria is specious because it was antipoverty measures, rather than the use of DDT, that eradicated malaria in the United States in the twentieth century.

3. DDT Use Must Be Combined with Other Measures to Control Malaria 59

Josie Glausiusz

While limited use of DDT can successfully reduce rates of malarial infection, evidence on the pesticide's long-term effects is uncertain, and it should not be used exclusively against the disease because of the tendency of malaria-carrying mosquitoes to develop DDT resistance.

4. Bed Nets Should Be Distributed to the
   Poor Free of Charge   66

   Awash Teklehaimanot, Jeffrey D. Sachs,
   and Chris Curtis

   The promotion of social marketing as a way to
   get antimalarial bed nets and drugs to affected
   communities has failed and must be replaced with
   a global policy of free distribution.

5. Bed Nets and Antimalaria Medications
   Should Be Distributed to the Poor at a
   Subsidized Cost   77

   UNICEF

   Financial support from Western nations has made
   impoverished countries where malaria is endemic
   overly dependent on aid and unable to deal with
   public health problems on their own.

6. Malaria Is One of Many Diseases That Will
   Resurge with Climate Change   82

   World Health Organization

   Global warming, which results in increased rainfall,
   temperatures, and humidity, has the potential to
   cause a resurgence of malaria and other insect-
   carried diseases in parts of the world where the
   condition was thought to be under control, as well
   as to increase the incidence in regions where malaria
   already thrives.

7. Global Climate Change Will Not Influence the
   Incidence of Malaria   87

   Paul Reiter

   Factors influencing the rise of malaria include
   deforestation, drug resistance, changes in
   agricultural practices, and resistance to insecticides,
   but do not include climate change.

8. The Effects of Global Warming on Diseases
   Such as Malaria Are Still Unclear   93

Maria Said

Many factors influence where and how quickly
diseases spread, including but not limited to climate
change, but researchers are not certain that global
warming will cause a widespread dispersion of
malaria.

CHAPTER **3**   The Personal Side of Malaria

1. Lack of Money Is the Most Common
   Issue Prohibiting Parents from Treating
   Their Children   100

Mark Dlugash

Families in malaria-endemic countries like Uganda
tend to be large, with parents earning as little as a
dollar a day, making it nearly impossible for them
to afford preventive measures such as bed nets or to
treat each of their children with every outbreak.

2. A Philanthropist Explains That Eradicating
   Malaria Will Take Investment and Innovation   108

Bill Gates, interviewed by Kristi Heim

Microsoft founder Bill Gates has donated $1 billion
and joined with notable scientists and technologists
to develop the world's first malaria vaccine.

3. Mothers Take Extreme Measures to Save
   Their Children from Malaria   117

Amy Ellis

Women in malaria-endemic countries often must
defy their husbands in order to obtain medical care
for their children.

4. Western Scientists Witness the Scourge of
   Malaria in African Countries   122
   Rebekah Kent
   Scientists and doctors working in malaria-endemic
   countries witness the effects of malaria firsthand,
   sometimes directly assisting in the aid of malaria
   victims.

5. One Man's Belief in Modern Medicine
   to Treat Malaria Sets an Example for
   His Village   127
   Voices for a Malaria-Free Future
   Individual families can influence and encourage
   their neighbors to use modern health clinics in
   small villages, potentially saving their children's
   lives.

Glossary   132
Chronology   134
Organizations to Contact   140
For Further Reading   144
Index   146

FOREWORD

"Medicine, to produce health, has to examine disease."
—Plutarch

Independent research on a health issue is often the first step to complement discussions with a physician. But locating accurate, well-organized, understandable medical information can be a challenge. A simple Internet search on terms such as "cancer" or "diabetes," for example, returns an intimidating number of results. Sifting through the results can be daunting, particularly when some of the information is inconsistent or even contradictory. The Greenhaven Press series Perspectives on Diseases and Disorders offers a solution to the often overwhelming nature of researching diseases and disorders.

From the clinical to the personal, titles in the Perspectives on Diseases and Disorders series provide students and other researchers with authoritative, accessible information in unique anthologies that include basic information about the disease or disorder, controversial aspects of diagnosis and treatment, and first-person accounts of those impacted by the disease. The result is a well-rounded combination of primary and secondary sources that, together, provide the reader with a better understanding of the disease or disorder.

Each volume in Perspectives on Diseases and Disorders explores a particular disease or disorder in detail. Material for each volume is carefully selected from a wide range of sources, including encyclopedias, journals, newspapers, nonfiction books, speeches, government documents, pamphlets, organization newsletters, and position papers. Articles in the first chapter provide an authoritative, up-to-date overview that covers symptoms, causes and effects, treatments, cures, and medical advances. The second chapter presents a substantial number of opposing viewpoints on controversial treatments and other current debates relating to the volume topic. The third chapter offers a variety of personal perspectives on the disease or disorder. Patients, doctors, caregivers, and loved ones represent just some of the voices found in this narrative chapter.

Each Perspectives on Diseases and Disorders volume also includes:

- An **annotated table of contents** that provides a brief summary of each article in the volume.
- An **introduction** specific to the volume topic.
- Full-color **charts and graphs** to illustrate key points, concepts, and theories.
- Full-color **photos** that show aspects of the disease or disorder and enhance textual material.
- **"Fast Facts"** that highlight pertinent additional statistics and surprising points.
- A **glossary** providing users with definitions of important terms.
- A **chronology** of important dates relating to the disease or disorder.
- An annotated list of **organizations to contact** for students and other readers seeking additional information.
- A **bibliography** of additional books and periodicals for further research.
- A detailed **subject index** that allows readers to quickly find the information they need.

Whether a student researching a disorder, a patient recently diagnosed with a disease, or an individual who simply wants to learn more about a particular disease or disorder, a reader who turns to Perspectives on Diseases and Disorders will find a wealth of information in each volume that offers not only basic information, but also vigorous debate from multiple perspectives.

INTRODUCTION

In 1955 the World Health Organization (WHO) undertook a massive public health campaign with the goal of eliminating malaria once and for all. Central to the project was the use of the synthetic chemical DDT, whose insecticidal properties had been discovered almost by accident in 1939 by a Swiss scientist named Paul Hermann Müller. Other infectious diseases such as typhus, cholera, and smallpox had been more or less controlled by the middle of the twentieth century, but malaria remained a serious health threat throughout much of the world, particularly in countries near the equator. DDT combated malaria by killing mosquitoes, the carriers of the parasite that causes malaria. DDT had been credited with eradicating malaria in the United States by 1951, although in reality its effectiveness was just one factor in the large-scale New Deal plan to stimulate economic growth during the Great Depression. Decades later it would be revealed that the simple act of encouraging people to put screens on their windows had probably been more effective at curbing malarial infection in the United States than insecticide use. Nevertheless, DDT was hailed at the time as one of the greatest developments in malaria prevention that the world had yet seen. Its use had a great impact during World War II after tens of thousands of Allied forces contracted malaria in the South Pacific and the Allies responded by spraying the region with DDT to combat the high rates of infection among the troops.

So it was with these successes in mind that WHO began its seemingly monumental task of coordinating a global malaria campaign. One of the early target countries was the island nation of Borneo in Indonesia, which had a significant incidence of malaria infection in some of its more remote villages. The plan advanced by WHO to address Borneo's malaria problem was a program of indoor residual spraying (IRS) of houses and other buildings, along with aerial spraying—both using DDT and other synthetic insecticides. The desired decline in malarial infection was achieved, but the program's wholly unexpected side effects led to bizarre events that have become a source of wild speculation and suspected myth for more than four decades. Details of the story change depending on the source, but its core elements are factual. Borneo was at the time, it seems, home to many cats, which began to die off after they had ingested DDT by licking themselves after rubbing against the walls of the sprayed buildings. With no more cats in the sprayed villages, the rat population exploded, destroying crops and threaten-

In America DDT spraying to combat malaria began in the 1940s, and malaria was eliminated in the United States by 1951. (Loomis Dean/Time Life Pictures/Getty Images)

ing residents with outbreaks of typhus. WHO responded by enlisting the Singapore Royal Air Force to parachute containers of cats rounded up from elsewhere on the island into the affected villages in an unlikely effort called Operation Cat Drop.

Reports of the Operation Cat Drop story were initially published several years after the 1960 cat transport, and it contained details that likely were added to embellish the potentially devastating consequences of introducing a foreign substance into an environment without regard to its long-term role in nature and its impact on the food chain. One version of the story held that more than fourteen thousand cats were dropped into the villages. The actual number was likely closer to two or three dozen, although there is written evidence of only one cat drop. According to the April/June 2005 issue of the *Quarterly News of the Association of Former WHO Staff*, the flight manifest from a March 1960 delivery mission by the Royal Air Force cites the transportation of twenty cats, locked in baskets and dropped via parachute over villages, with the notation, "Very accurate dropping." A more complex chain-of-events theory holds that the DDT poisoned parasitic flies, which were eaten by geckoes, which were in turn poisoned and eaten by the cats, which were also poisoned. But this is thought to have been added in the wake of the 1962 publication of Rachel Carson's *Silent Spring*, which essentially launched the modern environmental movement and brought to public awareness the dangers of DDT—including its high toxicity to a range of animals, especially fish and birds, and its suspected involvement in cancers, as well as neurological and developmental irregularities, in humans. Research into the effects of DDT over the last few decades indicates that the pesticide may not be as dangerous as initially feared, and while its use is still banned in most developed countries it continues to be part of the arsenal against malaria in much of the developing world.

Regardless of its details, the Operation Cat Drop story illustrates the difficulties inherent in confronting malaria. Having existed in one form or another for 30 to 60 million years, the malaria parasite is particularly cunning and mutates easily to ensure its own survival. According to pathogen researcher Karen Day of Oxford University, there are more than 160 species of the *Plasmodium* parasite, four of which infect humans, including the deadly *Plasmodium falciparum* that accounts for 80 percent of all malaria cases and 90 percent of deaths from malaria each year. Falciparum malaria began evolving around 5 to 7 million years ago, at about the same time early human ancestors broke off into a separate species from other hominid primates such as chimpanzees. The work performed on the *Plasmodium* genome sequence by a team of researchers at the University of California, Irvine, however, indicates that

British army physician Ronald Ross first proposed in the 1890s that mosquitoes were a carrier of malaria. **(Topical Press Agency/ Hulton Archive/Getty Images)**

the specific form of the falciparum malaria that infects humans today may be as little as six thousand years old—fifty-seven thousand years at the high end—coinciding with the development of agriculture in Africa. The British biomedical research foundation Wellcome Trust, which funds some of the *Plasmodium* genome research, asserts:

> This was a time of massive ecological change, when humans began living in large communities and the rainforest was being cut down for slash-and-burn agriculture. Other findings also support the timeframe for the birth of the modern *falciparum:* there was also a major change in the mosquito vector at that time, when it began biting humans instead of animals; and a human red blood cell polymorphism that protects against *falciparum* dates to less than 10,000 years ago.

Likewise, some scientists believe today's falciparum malaria may be far more deadly than its earlier incarnations, possibly due to the adaptation of more efficient biting by mosquitoes or shifts in population density that put more humans in areas with larger numbers of mosquitoes. And the *Anopheles* genus of mosquito is unique in that it has adapted to live among humans and feed exclusively on their blood.

Malaria's ability to evade efforts to stamp it out has frustrated the medical and scientific community since British army physician Ronald Ross first proposed that mosquitoes were the disease vector in the 1890s. With environmentalism a major global movement and malaria as big a threat as ever, activists on both sides have taken a strong stance on DDT. It is just one of the many battlegrounds in humanity's long fight against malaria.

CHAPTER 1

Understanding Malaria

An Overview of Malaria

Carol A. Turkington and Rebecca J. Frey

In the following viewpoint the authors explain that malaria exists primarily in developing countries with insufficient infrastructure and impoverished populations, but it is also becoming increasingly common within the borders of the United States, particularly as international travel grows in popularity, more immigrants enter the country, and overseas adoptions become more common. Malaria infection is caused by mosquitoes carrying any of four malaria parasites and is characterized by a high fever and chills, sweating, fatigue, headache, and nausea, which, if left untreated, can cause acute anemia, organ failure, and brain damage, among other problems. Malaria can be treated and cured, but because the parasite has developed resistance to many of the standard treatments, it is becoming more difficult for researchers to stay ahead of malaria. Sleeping under an insecticide-treated bed net remains one of the most effective preventive measures against the disease. Turkington and Frey are health and medical writers.

Photo on previous page. The female *Anopheles gambiae* feeds on human blood. Mosquitoes use the blood for egg production, but it may also carry the malaria infection. (Sinclair Stammers/Photo Researchers, Inc.)

SOURCE: Carol A. Turkington and Rebecca J. Frey, "Malaria," *Gale Encyclopedia of Medicine,* January 1, 2006. Reproduced by permission of Gale, a part of Cengage Learning.

Malaria is a growing problem in the United States. Although only about 1400 new cases were reported in the United States and its territories in 2000, many involved returning travelers. In addition, locally transmitted malaria has occurred in California, Florida, Texas, Michigan, New Jersey, and New York City. While malaria can be transmitted in blood, the American blood supply is not screened for malaria. Widespread malarial epidemics are far less likely to occur in the United States, but small localized epidemics could return to the Western world. As of late 2002, primary care physicians are being advised to screen returning travelers with fever for malaria, and a team of public health doctors in Minnesota is recommending screening immigrants, refugees, and international adoptees for the disease—particularly those from high-risk areas.

The picture is far more bleak, however, outside the territorial boundaries of the United States. A recent government panel warned that disaster looms over Africa from the disease. Malaria infects between 300 and 500 million people every year in Africa, India, southeast Asia, the Middle East, Oceania, and Central and South America. A 2002 report stated that malaria kills 2.7 million people each year, more than 75 percent of them African children under the age of five. It is predicted that within five years, malaria will kill about as many people as does AIDS. As many as half a billion people worldwide are left with chronic anemia due to malaria infection. In some parts of Africa, people battle up to 40 or more separate episodes of malaria in their lifetimes. The spread of malaria is becoming even more serious as the parasites that cause malaria develop resistance to the drugs used to treat the condition. In late 2002, a group of public health researchers in Thailand reported that a combination treatment regimen involving two drugs known as dihydroartemisinin and azithromycin shows promise in treating multidrug-resistant malaria in southeast Asia.

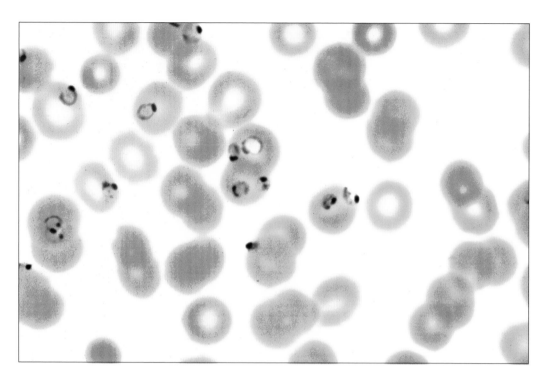

Of the four different species of parasites that cause malaria, *Plasmodium falciparum* is the most deadly and kills millions worldwide each year. (**Dr. Cecil H. Fox/Photo Researchers, Inc.**)

Causes of Malaria

Human malaria is caused by four different species of a parasite belonging to genus *Plasmodium*: *Plasmodium falciparum* (the most deadly), *Plasmodium vivax*, *Plasmodium malariae*, and *Plasmodium ovale*. The last two are fairly uncommon. Many animals can get malaria, but human malaria does not spread to animals. In turn, animal malaria does not spread to humans.

A person gets malaria when bitten by a female mosquito who is looking for a blood meal and is infected with the malaria parasite. The parasites enter the blood stream and travel to the liver, where they multiply. When they re-emerge into the blood, symptoms appear. By the time a patient shows symptoms, the parasites have reproduced very rapidly, clogging blood vessels and rupturing blood cells.

Malaria cannot be casually transmitted directly from one person to another. Instead, a mosquito bites an infected person and then passes the infection on to the next human it bites. It is also possible to spread malaria via contaminated needles or in blood transfusions. This is why all blood donors are carefully screened with questionnaires for possible exposure to malaria.

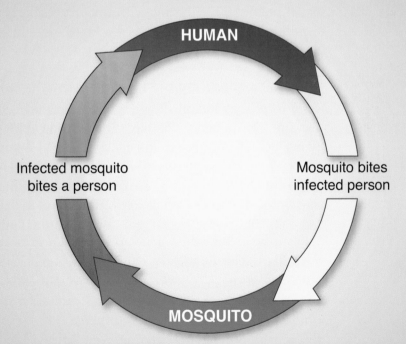

Complementary Roles Played by Humans and Mosquitoes in the Malaria Infection Cycle

Parasites multiply in human liver and bloodstream, causing malaria symptoms

HUMAN

Mosquito bites infected person

Infected mosquito bites a person

MOSQUITO

Parasites multiply in mosquito gut and migrate to salivary glands

Taken from: "What Is Malaria?" Roll Back Malaria Partnership. www.rollbackmalaria.org.

It is possible to contract malaria in non-endemic areas, although such cases are rare. Nevertheless, at least 89 cases of so-called airport malaria, in which travelers contract malaria while passing through crowded airport terminals, have been identified since 1969.

Symptoms of Malaria

The amount of time between the mosquito bite and the appearance of symptoms varies, depending on the strain of parasite involved. The incubation period is usually between 8 and 12 days for falciparum malaria, but it can be as long as a month for the other types. Symptoms from some strains of *P. vivax* may not appear until 8–10 months after the mosquito bite occurred.

The primary symptom of all types of malaria is the "malaria ague" (chills and fever). In most cases, the fever has three stages, beginning with uncontrollable shivering for an hour or two, followed by a rapid spike in temperature (as high as 106°F), which lasts three to six hours. Then, just as suddenly, the patient begins to sweat profusely, which will quickly bring down the fever. Other symptoms may include fatigue, severe headache, or nausea and vomiting. As the sweating subsides, the patient typically feels exhausted and falls asleep. In many cases, this cycle of chills, fever, and sweating occurs every other day, or every third day, and may last for between a week and a month. Those with the chronic form of malaria may have a relapse as long as 50 years after the initial infection.

Falciparum Malaria

Falciparum malaria is far more severe than other types of malaria because the parasite attacks all red blood cells, not just the young or old cells, as do other types. It causes the red blood cells to become very "sticky." A patient with this type of malaria can die within hours of the first symptoms, The fever is prolonged. So many red blood cells are destroyed that they block the blood vessels in vital organs (especially the kidneys), and the spleen becomes enlarged. There may be brain damage, leading to coma and convulsions. The kidneys and liver may fail.

Malaria in pregnancy can lead to premature delivery, miscarriage, or stillbirth.

Certain kinds of mosquitoes (called anopheles) can pick up the parasite by biting an infected human. (The more common kinds of mosquitoes in the United States do not transmit the infection.) This is true for as long as that human has parasites in his/her blood. Since strains of malaria do not protect against each other, it is possible to be reinfected with the parasites again and again. It is also possible to develop a chronic infection without developing an effective immune response.

Diagnosis of Malaria

Malaria is diagnosed by examining blood under a microscope. The parasite can be seen in the blood smears on a slide. These blood smears may need to be repeated over a 72-hour period in order to make a diagnosis. Antibody tests are not usually helpful because many people developed antibodies from past infections, and the tests may not be readily available. A new laser test to detect the presence of malaria parasites in the blood was developed in 2002, but is still under clinical study.

Two new techniques to speed the laboratory diagnosis of malaria show promise as of late 2002. The first is acridine orange (AO), a staining agent that works much faster (3–10 min) than the traditional Giemsa stain (45–60 min) in making the malaria parasites visible under a microscope. The second is a bioassay technique that measures the amount of a substance called histadine-rich protein II (HRP2) in the patient's blood. It allows for a very accurate estimation of parasite development. A dip strip that tests for the presence of HRP2 in blood samples appears to be more accurate in diagnosing malaria than standard microscopic analysis.

Anyone who becomes ill with chills and fever after being in an area where malaria exists must see a doctor and mention their recent travel to endemic areas. A person with the above symptoms who has been in a high-risk area should insist on a blood test for malaria. The doctor may believe the symptoms are just the common flu virus. Malaria is often misdiagnosed by North American doctors who are not used to seeing the disease. Delaying treatment of falciparum malaria can be fatal.

Treatment

Falciparum malaria is a medical emergency that must be treated in the hospital. The type of drugs, the method of giving them, and the length of the treatment depend on where the malaria was contracted and how sick the patient is.

For all strains except falciparum, the treatment for malaria is usually chloroquine (Aralen) by mouth for three days. Those falciparum strains suspected to be resistant to chloroquine are usually treated with a combination of quinine and tetracycline. In countries where quinine resistance is developing, other treatments may include clinda-mycin (Cleocin), mefloquin (Lariam), or sulfadoxone/ pyrimethamine (Fansidar). Most patients receive an antibiotic for seven days. Those who are very ill may need intensive care and intravenous (IV) malaria treatment for the first three days.

Anyone who acquired falciparum malaria in the Dominican Republic, Haiti, Central America west of the Panama Canal, the Middle East, or Egypt can still be cured with chloroquine. Almost all strains of falciparum malaria in Africa, South Africa, India, and southeast Asia are now resistant to chloroquine. In Thailand and Cambodia, there are strains of falciparum malaria that have some resistance to almost all known drugs.

A patient with falciparum malaria needs to be hospitalized and given antimalarial drugs in different combinations and doses depending on the resistance of the strain. The patient may need IV fluids, red blood cell transfusions, kidney dialysis, and assistance breathing.

A drug called primaquine may prevent relapses after recovery from *P. vivax* or *P. ovale.* These relapses are caused by a form of the parasite that remains in the liver and can reactivate months or years later.

Another new drug, halofantrine, is available abroad. While it is licensed in the United States, it is not marketed in this country and it is not recommended by the Centers for Disease Control and Prevention in Atlanta.

Alternative Treatments

The Chinese herb qinghaosu (the Western name is artemisinin) has been used in China and southeast Asia to fight severe malaria, and became available in Europe in 1994. Because this treatment often fails, it is usually combined with another antimalarial drug (mefloquine) to boost its effectiveness. It is not available in the United States and other parts of the developed world due to fears of its toxicity, in addition to licensing and other issues.

A Western herb called wormwood (*Artemesia annua*) that is taken as a daily dose can be effective against malaria. Protecting the liver with herbs like goldenseal (*Hydrastis canadensis*), Chinese goldenthread (*Coptis chinensis*), and milk thistle (*Silybum marianum*) can be used as preventive treatment. Preventing mosquitoes from biting you while in the tropics is another possible way to avoid malaria.

As of late 2002, researchers are studying a traditional African herbal remedy against malaria. Extracts from *Microglossa pyrifolia*, a trailing shrub belonging to the daisy family (Asteraceae), show promise in treating drug-resistent strains of *P. falciparum.*

FAST FACT

Chloroquine is an early antimalarial drug first used in the 1940s, but it quickly lost its effectiveness against *Plasmodium falciparum,* the deadliest of the malaria parasites. It is still used throughout African countries, however, because of its affordability, despite being largely ineffective.

Prognosis and Prevention

If treated in the early stages, malaria can be cured. Those who live in areas where malaria is epidemic, however, can contract the disease repeatedly, never fully recovering between bouts of acute infection.

Several researchers are currently working on a malarial vaccine, but the complex life cycle of the malaria parasite makes it difficult. A parasite has much more genetic material than a virus or bacterium. For this reason, a successful vaccine has not yet been developed.

Malaria is an especially difficult disease to prevent by vaccination because the parasite goes through several separate stages. One recent promising vaccine appears to have protected up to 60% of people exposed to malaria. This was evident during field trials for the drug that were conducted in South America and Africa. It is not yet commercially available.

The World Health Association (WHO) has been trying to eliminate malaria for the past 30 years by controlling mosquitoes. Their efforts were successful as long as the pesticide DDT killed mosquitoes and antimalarial drugs cured those who were infected. Today, however, the problem has returned a hundredfold, especially in Africa. Because both the mosquito and parasite are now extremely resistant to the insecticides designed to kill them, governments are now trying to teach people to take antimalarial drugs as a preventive medicine and avoid getting bitten by mosquitoes.

A New Breed of Mosquito

A newer strategy as of late 2002 involves the development of genetically modified non-biting mosquitoes. A research team in Italy is studying the feasibility of this means of controlling malaria.

Travelers to high-risk areas should use insect repellant containing DEET for exposed skin. Because DEET is toxic in large amounts, children should not use a concentration higher than 35%. DEET should not be inhaled. It should not be rubbed onto the eye area, on any broken or irritated skin, or on children's hands. It should be thoroughly washed off after coming indoors.

Those who use the following preventive measures get fewer infections than those who do not:

- Between dusk and dawn, remain indoors in well-screened areas.
- Sleep inside pyrethrin or permethrin repellent–soaked mosquito nets.
- Wear clothes over the entire body.

Advice for Travelers

Anyone visiting endemic areas should take antimalarial drugs starting a day or two before they leave the United States. The drugs used are usually chloroquine or mefloquine. This treatment is continued through at least four weeks after leaving the endemic area. However, even those who take antimalarial drugs and are careful to avoid mosquito bites can still contract malaria.

International travelers are at risk for becoming infected. Most Americans who have acquired falciparum malaria were visiting sub-Saharan Africa; travelers in Asia and South America are less at risk. Travelers who stay in air conditioned hotels on tourist itineraries in urban or resort areas are at lower risk than backpackers, missionaries, and Peace Corps volunteers. Some people in western cities where malaria does not usually exist may acquire the infection from a mosquito carried onto a jet. This is called airport or runway malaria.

Malaria Is One of the Oldest and Deadliest Known Diseases

Michael Finkel

Malaria is thought to be one of the world's most enduring diseases, in existence longer than human beings. In fact, scientists believe dinosaurs may have suffered from it. In the following selection Michael Finkel suggests that, today, despite a worldwide effort in the 1950s to eradicate the disease—an effort that nearly succeeded before interest ran out and the project was abandoned—malaria has resurged and is now responsible for more deaths than any other parasitic disease. Unlike other contagious illnesses, however, the biology of malaria has not been amenable to the development of a vaccine to combat it. Finkel explains that numerous efforts have been launched, some with moderate rates of success, but so far a vaccination that provides at least 90 percent coverage eludes researchers. For *National Geographic* reporter Finkel, writing about malaria had a personal dimension: Finkel himself contracted the illness while traveling in northern Thailand in 2002.

SOURCE: Michael Finkel, "Stopping a Global Killer," *National Geographic*, July 2007. Reproduced by permission.

We live on a malarious planet. It may not seem that way from the vantage point of a wealthy country, where malaria is sometimes thought of, if it is thought of at all, as a problem that has mostly been solved, like smallpox or polio. In truth, malaria now affects more people than ever before. It's endemic to 106 nations, threatening half the world's population. In recent years, the parasite has grown so entrenched and has developed resistance to so many drugs that the most potent strains can scarcely be controlled. This year malaria will strike up to a half billion people. At least a million will die, most of them under age five, the vast majority living in Africa. That's more than twice the annual toll a generation ago.

Malaria Is More Deadly than Ever

The outcry over this epidemic, until recently, has been muted. Malaria is a plague of the poor, easy to overlook. The most unfortunate fact about malaria, some researchers believe, is that prosperous nations got rid of it. In the meantime, several distinctly unprosperous regions have reached the brink of total malarial collapse, virtually ruled by swarms of buzzing, flying syringes.

Only in the past few years has malaria captured the full attention of aid agencies and donors. The World Health Organization has made malaria reduction a chief priority. Bill Gates, who has called malaria "the worst thing on the planet," has donated hundreds of millions of dollars to the effort through the Bill and Melinda Gates Foundation. The [George W.] Bush Administration has pledged 1.2 billion dollars. Funds devoted to malaria have doubled since 2003. The idea is to disable the disease by combining virtually every known malaria-fighting technique, from the ancient (Chinese herbal medicines) to the old (bed nets) to the ultramodern (multidrug cocktails). At the same time, malaria researchers are pursuing a long-sought, elusive goal: a vaccine that would curb the disease for good.

Much of the aid is going to a few hard-hit countries scattered across sub-Saharan Africa. If these nations can beat back the disease, they'll serve as templates for the global antimalaria effort. And if they can't? Well, nobody in the malaria world likes to answer that question. . . .

Malaria is a confounding disease—often, it seems, contradictory to logic. Curing almost all malaria cases can be worse than curing none. Destroying fragile wetlands, in the world of malaria, is a noble act. Rachel Carson, the environmental icon, is a villain; her three-letter devil, DDT, is a savior. Carrying a gene for an excruciating and often fatal blood disorder, sickle-cell anemia, is a blessing, for it confers partial resistance to [*Plasmodium*] *falciparum* [the malaria parasite that causes 95 percent of malaria deaths]. Leading researchers at a hundred medical centers are working on antimalarial medicines, but a medicinal plant described 1,700 years ago may be the best remedy available. "In its ability to adapt and survive," says Robert Gwadz, who has studied malaria at the National Institutes of Health, near Washington, D.C., for almost 35 years, "the malaria parasite is a genius. It's smarter than we are."

Malaria Has a Long History

The disease has been with humans since before we were human. Our hominid ancestors almost certainly suffered from malaria. The parasite and the mosquito are both ancient creatures—the dinosaurs might have had malaria—and this longevity has allowed the disease ample time to exploit the vulnerabilities of an immune system. And not just ours. Mice, birds, porcupines, lemurs, monkeys, and apes catch their own forms of malaria. Bats and snakes and flying squirrels have malaria.

Few civilizations, in all of history, have escaped the disease. Some Egyptian mummies have signs of malaria. Hippocrates documented the distinct stages of the illness; Alexander the Great likely died of it, leading to the unraveling of the Greek Empire. Malaria may have stopped the armies of both Attila the Hun and Genghis Khan.

The disease's name comes from the Italian *mal'aria* meaning "bad air"; in Rome, where malaria raged for centuries, it was commonly believed that swamp fumes produced the illness. At least four popes died of it. It may have killed Dante, the Italian poet. George Washington suffered from malaria, as did Abraham Lincoln and Ulysses S. Grant. In the late 1800s, malaria was so bad in Washington, D.C., that one prominent physician lobbied—unsuccessfully—to erect a gigantic wire screen around the city. A million Union Army casualties in the U.S. Civil War are attributed to malaria, and in the Pacific theater of World War II casualties from the disease exceeded those from combat. Some scientists believe that one out of every two people who have ever lived have died of malaria.

FAST FACT

Between 1965 and 1970 the U.S. Army reported approximately forty thousand cases of malaria among its soldiers fighting in the Vietnam War; seventy-eight of those afflicted died of the disease.

The first widely known remedy was discovered in present-day Peru and Ecuador. It was the bark of the cinchona tree, a close cousin of coffee. Local people called the remedy *quina quina* (bark of barks)—and it was later distributed worldwide as quinine. Word of the medicine, spread by Jesuit missionaries, reached a malaria-ravaged Italy in 1632, and demand became overwhelming. Harvested by indigenous laborers and carried to the Pacific coast for shipment to Europe, the bark sold for a fortune.

Several expeditions were dispatched to bring seeds and saplings back to Europe. After arriving in South America, the quinine hunters endured a brutal trek through the snow-choked passes of the Andes and down into the cloud forests where the elusive tree grew. Many perished in the effort. And even if the quinine hunters didn't die, the plants almost always did. For 200 years, until the cinchona tree was finally established on plantations in India,

Sri Lanka, and Java, the only way to acquire the cure was directly from South America.

Quinine, which disrupts the malaria parasites' reproduction, has saved countless lives, but it has drawbacks. It is short-acting, and if taken too frequently can cause serious side effects, including hearing loss. In the 1940s, however, came the first of two extraordinary breakthroughs: A synthetic malaria medicine was introduced. The compound was named chloroquine, and it was inexpensive, safe, and afforded complete, long-lasting protection against all forms of malaria. In other words, it was a miracle.

Bark from the cinchona tree is dried using special equipment. The bark produces quinine, the first widely known remedy for malaria. (© **Hulton Deutsch Collection/Corbis**)

The second innovation was equally miraculous. Swiss chemist Paul Müller discovered the insecticidal power of a compound called dichloro-diphenyl-trichloroethane, better known as DDT. Müller was awarded the 1948 Nobel Prize in medicine for his discovery, for nothing in the history of insect control had ever worked like DDT. Microscopic amounts could kill mosquitoes for months, long enough to disrupt the cycle of malaria transmission. It lasted twice as long as the next best insecticide, and cost one-fourth as much.

An Attempt at Global Eradication

Armed with the twin weapons of chloroquine and DDT, the World Health Organization in 1955 launched the Global Malaria Eradication Programme. The goal was to eliminate the disease within ten years. More than a billion dollars was spent. Tens of thousands of tons of DDT were applied each year to control mosquitoes. India, where malaria had long been a plague, hired 150,000 workers, full-time, to spray homes. Chloroquine was widely distributed. It was probably the most elaborate international health initiative ever undertaken.

The campaign was inspired by early successes in Brazil and the United States. The U.S. had recorded millions of malaria cases during the 1930s, mostly in southern states. Then an intensive antimalaria program was launched. More than three million acres (1.2 million hectares) of wetlands were drained, DDT was sprayed in hundreds of thousands of homes, and in 1946 the Centers for Disease Control was founded in Atlanta specifically to combat malaria.

America's affluence was a major asset. Almost everyone could get to a doctor; windows could be screened; resources were available to bulldoze mosquito-breeding swamps. There's also the lucky fact that the country's two most common species of *Anopheles* mosquitoes prefer feeding on cattle rather than humans. By 1950, transmission of malaria was halted in the U.S.

Children and Malaria

More than 40 percent of the world's children live in malaria-endemic countries.

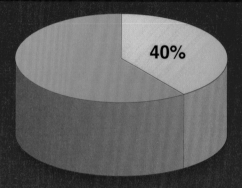

40%

More than 75 percent of the malaria infections worldwide occur in African children less than five years old.

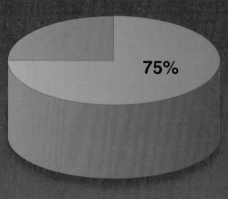

75%

Taken from: "Children and Malaria" Roll Back Malaria Partnership. www.rollbackmalaria.org.

The global eradication effort did achieve some notable successes. Malaria was virtually wiped out in much of the Caribbean and South Pacific, from the Balkans, from Taiwan. In Sri Lanka, there were 2.8 million cases of malaria in 1946, and a total of 17 in 1963. In India, malaria deaths plummeted from 800,000 a year to scarcely any.

But it was also clear that the campaign was far too ambitious. In much of the deep tropics malaria persisted stubbornly. Financing for the effort eventually withered, and the eradication program was abandoned in 1969. In many nations, this coincided with a decrease in foreign aid, with political instability and burgeoning poverty, and with overburdened public health services.

In several places where malaria had been on the brink of extinction, including both Sri Lanka and India, the disease came roaring back. And in much of sub-Saharan Africa, malaria eradication never really got started. The WHO program largely bypassed the continent, and smaller scale efforts made little headway.

Soon after the program collapsed, mosquito control lost access to its crucial tool, DDT. The problem was overuse—not by malaria fighters but by farmers, especially cotton growers, trying to protect their crops. The spray was so cheap that many times the necessary doses were sometimes applied. The insecticide accumulated in the soil and tainted watercourses. Though nontoxic to humans, DDT harmed peregrine falcons, sea lions, and salmon. In 1962 Rachel Carson published *Silent Spring*, documenting this abuse and painting so damning a picture that the chemical was eventually outlawed by most of the world for agricultural use. Exceptions were made for malaria control, but DDT became nearly impossible to procure. "The ban on DDT," says Gwadz of the National Institutes of Health, "may have killed 20 million children."

Then came the biggest crisis of all: widespread drug resistance. Malaria parasites reproduce so quickly that they evolve on fast-forward, constantly spinning out new mutations. Some mutations protected the parasites from chloroquine. The trait was swiftly passed to the next generation of parasites, and with each new exposure to chloroquine the drug-resistant parasites multiplied. Soon they were unleashing large-scale malaria epidemics for which treatment could be exceedingly difficult. By the 1990s, malaria afflicted a greater number of people, and was harder to cure than ever. . . .

The Difficulties of Developing a Vaccine

No matter how much time, money, and energy are expended on the effort, there still remains the most implacable of foes—biology itself. ACTs [artemisinin-based combination therapy drugs] are potent, but malaria experts fear that resistance may eventually develop, depriving doctors of their best tool. Before the ban on DDT, there were already scattered reports of *Anopheles* mosquitoes resistant to the insecticide; with its return, there are sure to be more. Meanwhile, global warming may be allowing the insects to colonize higher altitudes and farther latitudes.

Drugs, sprays, and nets, it appears, will never be more than part of the solution. What's required is an even more decisive weapon. "When I look at the whole malaria situation," says Louis Miller, co-chief of the malaria unit at the National Institute of Allergy and Infectious Diseases, "it all seems to come down to one basic idea: We sure need a vaccine."

It's easy to list every vaccine that can prevent a parasitic disease in humans. There is none. Vaccines exist for bacteria and viruses, but these are comparatively simple organisms. The polio virus, for example, consists of exactly 11 genes. *Plasmodium falciparum* has more than 5,000. It's this complexity, combined with the malaria parasite's constant motion—dodging like a fugitive from the mosquito to the human bloodstream to the liver to the red blood cells—that makes a vaccine fiendishly difficult to design.

Ideally, a malaria vaccine would provide lifelong protection. A lull in malaria transmission could cause many people to lose any immunity they have built up against the disease—even adults, immunologically speaking, could revert to infant status—rendering it more devastating if it returned. This is why a partial victory over malaria could be worse than total failure. *Falciparum* also has countless substrains (each river valley seems to have its own type), and a vaccine has to block them all. And of course the vaccine can leave no opening for the parasite to develop resistance. Creating a malaria vaccine is one of the most ambitious medical quests of all time.

Pregnant Women Are the Adult Group Most Vulnerable to Malaria

Women Deliver

Pregnant women are particularly vulnerable to malaria infection because pregnancy reduces immunity against the disease. Already subject to anemia as a side effect of pregnancy, women infected with malaria are even more likely to suffer from acute anemia, which is believed to cause approximately ten thousand deaths per year in malaria-endemic sub-Saharan Africa alone. Coexistence of HIV infection exacerbates the effects of malaria, and some malaria symptoms can mimic those of early pregnancy, making diagnosis difficult. Treatment also can be challenging, as not all antimalarial drugs have proven safe to use during pregnancy. Women's lack of decision-making power in the home and overall low social status in malaria-endemic countries increases their susceptibility to contracting malaria because they rarely possess the income or independence to purchase insecticide-treated bed nets or obtain medical care. The Women Deliver Initiative is a compendium of international advocacy groups working to make pregnancy and childbirth safer in the developing world.

SOURCE: "Pregnant Women Are Adult Group Most at Risk from Malaria," *Women Deliver Global Conference,* 2007. Reproduced by permission of Malaria Consortium and Women Deliver.

Malaria is a devastating disease with some 40 percent of the world's population in 107 countries at risk today. Pregnant women are the main adult group at risk of malaria and are four times more likely to suffer malaria than other adults. Every year an estimated 30 million women living in Africa's malaria-endemic countries become pregnant.

Pregnancy reduces a woman's immunity to malaria making her more likely to become infected/affected. Pregnant women's increased vulnerability to malaria can have devastating consequences for both the woman and her unborn child. In sub-Saharan Africa malaria infection is estimated to cause 400,000 cases of severe maternal anaemia which contributes significantly to maternal mortality—causing an estimated 10,000 deaths per year. Despite this, it is estimated that less than five percent of pregnant women have access to effective malaria interventions.

The unborn children of women with malaria are also affected and at greater risk of spontaneous abortion, still birth, premature delivery and low birth weight. Some 200,000 newborn deaths a year are estimated to be due to malaria in pregnancy. . . .

The problems that malaria infection causes during pregnancy differ depending on the type of malaria transmission area. For example, in high transmission areas where women have gained a level of immunity to malaria that is lessened during pregnancy, malaria infection is likely to result in severe maternal anaemia and delivery of low birth-weight infants. In areas of low transmission where women generally have developed no immunity to malaria infection during pregnancy infection is more likely to result in severe malaria disease, maternal anaemia, premature delivery, or stillbirth.

The burden of malaria in pregnancy is exacerbated by HIV infection, which increases susceptibility to malaria in pregnancy, reduces the effectiveness of antimalarial

Malaria Infection During Pregnancy Affects Mothers, Fetuses, and Newborns

Pregnant Woman
- parasitaemia
- anemia
- febrile illness
- cerebral malaria
- hypoglycemia
- severe disease
- hemorrhage

Fetus
- abortion
- stillbirth
- congenital infection

Newborn
- low birth weight
- prematurity
- intrauterine growth retardation
- malaria illness
- mortality

Taken from: World Health Organization, "A Strategic Framework for Malaria Prevention and Control During Pregnancy in the African Region." Brazzaville: WHO Regional Office for Africa, 2004.

interventions, and complicates the use of antimalarials because of potential drug interactions.

One of the difficulties in diagnosing malaria is that the disease-related symptoms can be easily confused with pregnancy-related symptoms.

Malaria Prevention and Treatment for Pregnant Women

Efforts to prevent malaria in pregnant women focus on sleeping under insecticide-treated nets (ITNs) and intermittent treatment with an antimalarial drug. ITNs decrease both the number of malaria cases and the number of malaria deaths in pregnant women and their children. Studies have shown that in areas where there are high rates of malaria, women protected by ITNs every night during their first four pregnancies give birth to 25 percent fewer underweight or premature newborns. Using ITNs also benefits infants who sleep under the net with their mother.

Intermittent preventive treatment (IPT) involves providing pregnant women with at least two preventative treatment doses of antimalarial drugs. Evidence shows this is a safe, inexpensive and effective way of preventing malaria during pregnancy with a decline in both infection rates, and in the number of low birth weight babies.

At the first African Summit on Malaria held in Abuja, Nigeria in 2000, African heads of state committed to providing effective malaria interventions to at least 60 percent of pregnant women by 2005.

> **FAST FACT**
>
> According to the World Health Organization, between 8 and 36 percent of pregnant women infected with malaria will give birth prematurely.

Malaria and Maternal Health Services

The World Health Organization (WHO) has introduced malaria guidelines into their Making Pregnancy Safer programme. Antenatal [prenatal] clinics are a key setting where women can be made aware of the problems of malaria and take preventative steps. However, whilst delivery of malaria interventions through antenatal clinics in malaria-endemic areas needs to be widespread, WHO acknowledges that currently this approach is the exception rather than the rule.

Pregnant women who do not attend antenatal clinics or who attend only for the first visit or too late during pregnancy need to be reached. Many women are not aware that pregnancy makes them more susceptible to malaria and new strategies are needed to encourage these women to attend antenatal care early and consistently.

Other challenges include drug resistance and the safe and appropriate use of different antimalarial drugs during pregnancy. As resistance to antimalarial drugs increases, the challenges of treatment and prevention of malaria among pregnant women become greater. Research in this area is therefore a high priority.

Effective management and treatment of malaria have also been hampered due to lack of research/development

In February 2008 President George W. Bush visits a Tanzanian garment factory where mosquito nets are made for distribution to pregnant African women to help prevent malaria. (**Mandel Ngan/ AFP/Getty Images**)

linked to issues of drug safety concerns for pregnant women which make companies reluctant to test drugs and treatments in pregnant women.

Gender and Malaria

Women are more vulnerable to malaria not only due to biological factors, but also due to socio-cultural and gender-based factors. In developing countries, women can be excluded from decisions on household purchases (e.g. ITNs) and their bargaining power within the household can significantly impact on their treatment-seeking behaviour and their ability to care for their health and that of their children.

Low social status, lack of access to formal education, poor nutrition and less access to financial resources are some of the key factors that increase women's vulnerability to malaria.

Gender inequality also has a direct impact on women's vulnerability to HIV with women accounting for a majority of HIV infections in sub-Saharan Africa, and heightens the risk of co-infection with malaria.

Empowering women is essential for reducing their vulnerability to malaria, and ensuring that women have a greater voice in household and community decisions is critical to fulfilling the rights of children.

A Malaria Vaccine Shows Promise

Jean Stéphenne

In collaboration with the Bill & Melinda Gates Foundation and the PATH Malaria Vaccine Initiative, an international group of research scientists at the pharmaceutical company GlaxoSmithKline have tested a potential malaria vaccine showing a 53 percent rate of success in preventing malaria in children five to seventeen months of age. In the following viewpoint Jean Stéphenne says that, despite limited potential for profitability, the company is committed to developing the vaccine for widespread use in developing countries where malaria is endemic. The company states that cooperation in the project from World Bank donor countries is essential, however, and large-scale investments in health care infrastructure must take place if a vaccine is to be created and made widely available in the poorest countries. Stéphenne is president and general manager of GlaxoSmithKline Biologicals.

SOURCE: Jean Stéphenne, "Defeat Malaria? Yes We Can," *Wall Street Journal*, December 17, 2008.

L ast week [in early December 2008], two studies published in the *New England Journal of Medicine* reported promising news about a malaria vaccine candidate that our company, GlaxoSmithKline, is developing in collaboration with the Malaria Vaccine Initiative, a program of the nonprofit organization PATH, the Bill & Melinda Gates Foundation, and scientists from across Europe, North America and Africa.

The studies focused on the most vulnerable populations in Kenya and Tanzania. One study reported that the vaccine candidate was 53% effective in preventing episodes of clinical malaria in children five to 17 months old. The second study demonstrated that the vaccine candidate can be administered alongside the standard set of vaccines used in national immunization programs for young infants.

These positive results help pave the way for the pivotal Phase III efficacy study that will recruit up to 16,000 children and infants at 11 trial sites in seven countries. If successful, that trial—the largest malaria vaccine trial in Africa's history—could lead to regulatory filing in 2011. The vaccine is designed to help complement existing malaria control measures, like mosquito nets, in Africa.

A Humanitarian Effort

Why would a company like ours devote 25 years of research and more than $300 million of shareholders' capital to develop a malaria vaccine? After all, there has never been a vaccine against *any* parasitic disease. Moreover, this vaccine is only relevant in some of the world's poorest countries, leaving little opportunity for profit.

We did it because it was the right thing to do. Malaria kills about one million African children a year and this vaccine can potentially save hundreds of thousands of lives, and avert billions of dollars in economic losses.

With a $29 million grant from the Bill & Melinda Gates Foundation, the Life Science and Translational Research Center has opened a malaria vaccine manufacturing facility in Rockville, Maryland. (Brendan Smialowski/ Getty Images)

Partnerships have been crucial to this endeavor. Our initial partner in the mid-1980s was the U.S. Walter Reed Army Institute of Research, which needed a malaria vaccine to protect troops who might be deployed to malaria-endemic regions. When data showed that the vaccine could best protect infants and children, we enlisted our current partners, who have helped shoulder some of the financial risks. Consistent with our commitment to making vaccines available to all those who need them, we have pledged that price will not be a barrier to the vaccine's implementation. This is "creative capitalism," as Bill Gates has called it, at its best.

Investment in Health Care Is Essential

But this is not the end of the story. We, as a global community, need to be creative in ensuring that *all* lifesaving vaccines reach those who need them most. Especially during these tough economic times, we must resist calls to cut back on investments in global health, which are crucial to saving lives and promoting economic growth.

One thing is clear: We can't do it alone. We in industry do not pretend to have all the answers. If this malaria vaccine demonstrates efficacy in the Phase III trial, we will need the help of many partners to distribute it to all of the children who need it. This means working closely with the World Health Organization, UNICEF, the World Bank, the GAVI Alliance, Roll Back Malaria, the Global Fund to Fight AIDS, TB and Malaria, the European and African Unions and others to ensure that funding and on-the-ground infrastructure are in place to allow swift uptake.

The good news is that in recent years the global community has set up new, effective mechanisms for financing vaccines for the poorest. For example, a new concept, called the Advance Market Commitment—a binding pledge by government agencies and other donors to purchase vaccines under development—is being developed with the World Bank and leading donor countries. The challenge for the next few years is to design a financing mechanism for malaria and to integrate it with malaria control programs and pediatric immunizations.

> **FAST FACT**
>
> All existing vaccines prevent either bacterial infections, such as tetanus and pertussis, or viral infections, such as polio and smallpox. Because malaria is caused by a parasite, development of a safe and effective vaccine has eluded researchers for decades.

Success Is the Only Option

In this respect, the vaccine candidate cleared a big hurdle with the news it could be safely and effectively co-administered when babies get their standard immunizations. That should go a long way to reassure those who

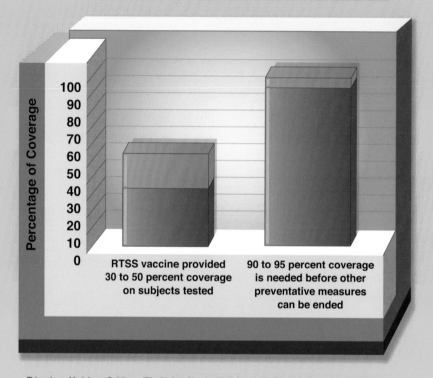

Effectiveness of Experimental RTSS Malaria Vaccine, 2008

Percentage of Coverage

100
90
80
70
60
50
40
30
20
10
0

RTSS vaccine provided
30 to 50 percent coverage
on subjects tested

90 to 95 percent coverage
is needed before other
preventative measures
can be ended

Taken from: Mark Leon Goldberg, "The Malaria Vaccine Explained," *UN Dispatch*, December 11, 2008.

are worried about the practicality of providing another new vaccine in resource-poor settings.

So whenever I'm asked whether we as a global community are up to the challenge—whether we can continue to develop and deploy desperately needed vaccines during difficult economic times—I never hesitate to answer. Citing the words of Kenya's most famous son [Barack Obama], I reply: "Yes, we can." For the sake of Africa's children, we must.

CHAPTER 2

Controversies Surrounding Malaria Prevention and Treatment

African Countries Must Have Access to DDT to Eradicate Malaria

Sam Zaramba

In the following viewpoint author Sam Zaramba contends that while wealthy Western countries have largely succeeded in eradicating malaria, they have continued to treat African countries as colonies, denying them access to the chemical insecticide DDT because of misplaced environmental concerns. In reality, more than 10 million people per year are infected with malaria in Uganda alone, making DDT use imperative if the disease is to be successfully combated. When DDT spraying programs were implemented in Uganda, the country saw a 90 percent drop in its population's reliance on antimalarial drugs and public health services, allowing a huge surge in work and school attendance. With careful handling and use, DDT not only is not harmful but in fact will save countless African lives. Zaramba is Uganda's director general of health services.

Photo on previous page. Since World War II, the use of DDT to control malaria in African countries has been controversial. (© Bettmann/Corbis)

Though Africa's sad experience with colonialism ended in the 1960s, a lethal vestige [trace] remains: malaria. It is the biggest killer of Ugandan

SOURCE: Sam Zaramba, "Give Us DDT," *Wall Street Journal,* June 12, 2007. © 2007 Dow Jones & Company. All rights reserved. Reprinted with permission of The Wall Street Journal and the author.

and all African children. Yet it remains preventable and curable. Last week [in early June 2007] in Germany, G-8 [group of eight developed countries] leaders committed new resources to the fight against the mosquito-borne disease and promised to use every available tool.

Now they must honor this promise by supporting African independence in the realm of disease control. We must be able to use Dichloro-Diphenyl-Trichloroethane—DDT.

The United States and Europe eradicated malaria by 1960, largely with the use of DDT. At the time, Uganda tested the pesticide in the Kanungu district and reduced malaria by 98%. Despite this success, we lacked the resources to sustain the program. Rather than partner with us to improve our public health infrastructure, however, foreign donors blanched. They used Africa's lack of infrastructure to justify not investing in it.

Today, every single Ugandan still remains at risk. Over 10 million Ugandans are infected each year, and up to 100,000 of our mothers and children die from the disease. Recently Ugandan country music star Job Paul Kafeero died of the disease, a reminder that no one is beyond its reach. Yet, many still argue that Africa's poor infrastructure makes indoor spraying too costly and complex a means of fighting malaria.

> **FAST FACT**
>
> Rachel Carson (1907–1964) was an American biologist and ecologist who became alarmed by the overuse of chemical pesticides, specifically DDT. Her 1962 book, *Silent Spring*, became a seminal publication in the environmental movement.

Uganda Tests Insecticide Use

Uganda is one of a growing number of African countries proving these people wrong. In 2006, Uganda worked with [former U.S.] President George [W.] Bush's Malaria Initiative to train 350 spray operators, supervisors and health officials. In August 2006 and again in February 2007, we covered 100,000 households in the southern Kabale district with the insecticide Icon. Nearly everyone welcomed this protection. The prevalence of the malaria parasite dropped. Today, just 3% of the local population carries the disease, down from 30%.

President George W. Bush speaks at the White House Summit on Malaria about his initiative to train technicians for spraying DDT in Uganda. (AP Images)

This exercise pays for itself. With 90% fewer people requiring anti-malarial medication and other public-health resources, more healthy adults work and more children attend school. When we repeated the test program in Kabale and neighboring Kanungu district [in 2007], our spray teams required little new training and were rapidly mobilized. Our health officials at every level were able to educate our communities, implement spraying programs and evaluate operations. With each passing year, it will now be easier and less expensive to run the programs.

But DDT lasts longer, costs less and is more effective against malaria-carrying mosquitoes than Icon. It functions as a spatial repellent to keep mosquitoes out of homes, as an irritant to prevent them from biting, and as a toxic agent to kill those that land. The repellency effect works without physical contact. And because we will never use the chemical in agriculture, DDT also makes mosquitoes less likely to develop resistance.

WHO Supports DDT Use

The U.S. banned DDT in 1972, spurred on by environmentalist Rachel Carson's 1962 book *Silent Spring*. Many countries in Europe and around the world followed suit. But after decades of exhaustive scientific review, DDT has been shown to not only be safe for humans and the environment, but also the single most effective anti-malarial agent ever invented. Nothing else at any price does everything it can do. That is why the World Health Organization (WHO) has once again recommended using DDT wherever possible against malaria, alongside insecticidal nets and effective drugs.

We are trying to do precisely this. In addition to distributing nearly three million long-lasting insecticidal nets and 25 million doses of effective anti-malarial drugs, we will expand our indoor spraying operations to four more districts this year, where we will protect tens of thousands of Ugandans from malaria's deadly scourge. We are committed to storing, transporting and using DDT properly in these programs, in accord with the Stockholm Convention, WHO, European Union and U.S. Agency for International Development guidelines. We are working with these organizations and to ensure support from our communities, and to ensure that our agricultural trade is not jeopardized.

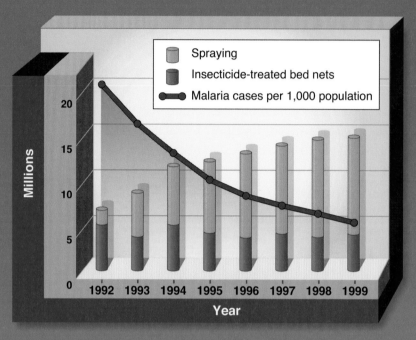

Malaria Cases Fell as Prevention Rose Between 1992 and 1999 in Vietnam

Legend:
- Spraying
- Insecticide-treated bed nets
- Malaria cases per 1,000 population

Taken from: World Health Organization, "Coming to Grips with Malaria in the New Millennium," United Nations Development Programme, 2005.

G-8 Must Accept DDT Use

Although Uganda's National Environmental Management Authority has approved DDT for malaria control, Western environmentalists continue to undermine our efforts and discourage G-8 governments from supporting us. The EU has acknowledged our right to use DDT, but some consumer and agricultural groups repeat myths and lies about the chemical. They should instead help us use it strictly to control malaria.

Environmental leaders must join the 21st century, acknowledge the mistakes Carson made, and balance the hypothetical risks of DDT with the real and devastating consequences of malaria. Uganda has demonstrated that, with the proper support, we can conduct model indoor spraying programs and ensure that money is spent wisely, chemicals are handled properly, our program responds promptly to changing conditions, and malaria is brought under control.

Africa is determined to rise above the contemporary colonialism that keeps us impoverished. We expect strong leadership in G-8 countries to stop paying lip service to African self-determination and start supporting solutions that are already working.

DDT Was Never Successful in Eradicating Malaria

Sonia Shah

According to viewpoint author Sonia Shah, the argument that wide-spread availability of DDT in African countries will eradicate malaria is false. While proponents contend that the Centers for Disease Control's [CDC's] DDT-spraying campaign from 1947 to 1951 successfully eradicated the disease in the United States, they fail to note that incidence of the disease actually had begun to taper off in the late 1920s and was only a real public-health threat in areas of the deep South into the 1930s, at which point the actions of the Tennessee Valley Authority finally ended the malaria threat in the United States. It was only after World War II, when authorities feared American soldiers returning from service overseas would reintroduce malaria to the country, that the CDC instituted a preventive spraying campaign. In reality, DDT use to combat malaria was less than effective because malaria-carrying mosquitoes became resistant to the pesticide, and DDT's dangers were already known to government scientists before Rachel Carson published her book, *Silent Spring*. The best tactic for combating malaria in Africa is not more pesticide use but improved infrastructure and the reduction of extreme poverty. Shah is an investigative journalist who writes frequently about the intersection of politics and health in developing countries.

SOURCE: Sonia Shah, "Don't Blame Environmentalists for Malaria," *Nation*, March 31, 2006. Reproduced by permission of the author.

Tina Rosenberg's long opinion piece on the *New York Times* website brings much-needed attention to the plight of "poor people's diseases," from sleeping sickness to tuberculosis ("The 'Scandal of Poor People's Diseases,'" *Times Select*, March 29 [2006]). But her argument about malaria—that more DDT would vanquish the disease—is all wrong.

The basic gist of the argument is thus: Americans wiped out malaria using DDT, but because über-green [author and environmentalist] Rachel Carson crusaded against the insecticide in *Silent Spring,* we self-righteously deprived the rest of the world of the miracle toxin. Two conclusions can be drawn from this little tale. One: Post-Carson environmentalists have the blood of Africans dripping from their hands. Two: To quote from the title of a previous Rosenberg story on the subject, "What the world needs now is DDT."

There are several problems with this story. The first is that DDT didn't wipe out malaria in the United States. The Centers for Disease Control's door-to-door DDT spray campaign of 1947–1951 was not about eradicating malaria in the United States, because malaria was already gone. The US Public Health Service had noted the "diminishing menace" of malaria in the United States by 1928—seventeen years before DDT showed up on the scene. The pockets of malaria that persisted in the South until the late 1930s were finally vanquished by the swamp-draining, electricity-giving activities of the Tennessee Valley Authority, which cut down on mosquito breeding sites and enabled locals to start living in well-screened houses. The rationale behind the DDT spray campaign was to prevent the re-introduction of

FAST FACT

The Tennessee Valley Authority was created by U.S. president Franklin Roosevelt in 1933 as part of his New Deal plan to revive the economy during the Great Depression. Its mandate was innovative resource management throughout the Tennessee Valley region, which included bringing electricity to rural areas, combating soil erosion, and ending deaths from malaria.

malaria from troops returning home from World War II. About the best one CDC physician involved in the campaign could say about it was that "we kicked a dying dog."

Timeline of Mosquito Resistance to Various Chemical Pesticides in California, 1945–1968

1945

DDT use begins in California to combat mosquitoes.

1961

Mosquitoes in California develop resistance to DDT; scientists create ethyl parathion.

1963

California mosquitoes develop resistance to ethyl parathion; scientists develop methyl parathion, which also fails.

1968

Synthetic insecticide fenthion is halted when mosquitoes in California develop resistance.

Taken from: *Time*, "Mending Mosquitoes," October 12, 1970.

DDT Resistance Is to Blame

The second problem is that the world did try to wipe out malaria using DDT. That campaign, launched by the WHO in 1955, eradicated malaria from a few marginal areas in Southern Europe and a couple of islands. But in places where malaria reigned supreme, it failed miserably. That isn't because they didn't have enough DDT but because the stuff stopped working. Malarial mosquitoes resistant to DDT cousin Dieldrin emerged in Nigeria as early as 1955. Malarial mosquitoes in Venezuela had learned to simply avoid DDT-sprayed walls and bite people outside by 1957. By 1972, when the United States finally banned DDT, nineteen species of malarial mosquitoes had already become impervious to the toxin.

The third problem is that Rachel Carson and the enviros who followed her were not the sole critics of DDT. By the time Carson wrote *Silent Spring* in 1962, concerns about DDT had been circulating among government experts for years. Not one month after DDT's launch in the consumer market in September 1947, experts were calling DDT "injurious to birds," according to the *New York Times*. "Experts warn new insecticide also may be fatal to fish—further tests urged," the *Times* headline read. USDA [United States Department of Agriculture] scientists were urging Congress to ban DDT use on dairy animals by May 1947.

End Poverty to Eradicate Malaria

Finally, it is true that environmental groups initially supported a UN-led worldwide ban on DDT in 2000. But they quickly about-faced when informed about its use—albeit limited—in malaria control. "You can only accuse them of naïveté," says malaria expert Amir Attaran. Not so chemical giant Bayer. "We fully support EU to ban imports of agricultural products coming from countries using DDT," wrote Bayer's Gerhard Hesse in an e-mail message leaked to the *Financial Times* last year [2005].

Rachel Carson's 1962 book, *Silent Spring,* was critical of the use of DDT. However, says the viewpoint's author, concerns about its use had been under discussion among government experts for years prior to publication of Carson's book. **(Alfred Eisenstaedt/ Time Life Pictures/Getty Images)**

Chemical giant Bayer manufactures brand-name insecticides much pricier than cheap, off-patent DDT. "DDT use for us is a commercial threat," Hesse wrote.

The conclusion one might draw from the real story of DDT and malaria is clear. DDT may alleviate malaria in some places, sometimes, if it still works to repel malarial mosquitoes. That won't be true in many places. And so the "world" does not need more DDT. What the world needs is better housing and civil engineering—in short, an end to poverty. That's what wiped out malaria at home, and that's what will wipe it out elsewhere, too, along with a host of other ills.

DDT Use Must Be Combined with Other Measures to Control Malaria

Josie Glausiusz

The modern environmental movement was born after the 1962 publication of Rachel Carson's *Silent Spring*, which argued that synthetic chemical pesticides, especially DDT, were deadly to fish and birds and posed a serious threat to human health. Critics, however, have maintained that Carson's theory was exaggerated and even argue that the international ban on DDT has caused countless deaths as malaria has resurged in some regions. Josie Glausiusz reports in the following viewpoint that malaria researchers are particularly torn about the safety and effectiveness of using DDT to kill malaria-carrying mosquitoes. Some claim indoor spraying poses no threat to human health whatsoever and can only help prevent malaria infection, while others are more cautious because reliable data are not available to study the effectiveness of DDT in developing countries. Nevertheless, apparently successful spraying programs in some countries, including South Africa, appear to show that DDT can be used successfully as part of a widespread effort to control the spread of malaria. In that country, the number of malaria cases dropped by 65 percent and the number of deaths from the disease by 73 percent in the two years DDT was used alongside artemisinin, a drug that fights malaria infections. However, a combined approach of "integrated vector management" is believed to be the most promising strategy to eliminate malaria. Glausiusz is a science writer whose works have appeared in publications such as *Discover*, *Wired*, and *Nature*.

SOURCE: Josie Glausiusz, "Can a Maligned Pesticide Save Lives?" *Discover*, November 20, 2007. Reproduced by permission.

DDT, formerly one of the most common industrial chemicals, was banned in the United States three decades ago, in no small part due to the work of one woman: Rachel Carson. Born a century ago this year [2007], Carson published *Silent Spring*, a haunting book that has been credited with helping to found the modern environmental movement in 1962. In her landmark book, she documented a litany of evils observed after DDT and other organochlorine insecticides were sprayed on landscapes, rivers, and lawns: dead birds and paralyzed birds, pigeons dropping from the sky, bird nests without eggs and eggs that did not hatch, dead fish and fish swimming in circles, cancers in humans, and a buildup of DDT in the fat of animals and people.

But in more recent years, a conglomeration of critics from organizations as diverse as the conservative American Enterprise Institute and the civil rights group Congress of Racial Equality have charged that Carson overstated the dangers of DDT, that it is not a carcinogen, and that at moderate doses, it is not even harmful to birds. Above all, her opponents argue that the reduction in DDT use has led to a dramatic rise in mosquito-borne malaria cases in Africa and South America. Bring back DDT, they demand, and let it be sprayed on the inner walls of houses, where it would kill vectors of malaria and other insect-borne diseases like dengue and typhus.

It's clear that eliminating DDT as a common agricultural pesticide has had marked environmental benefits, according to Chandler Robbins, an 89-year-old wildlife biologist at the U.S. Geological Survey's Patuxent Wildlife Research Center in Laurel, Maryland, who worked directly with Carson in the 1940s. (Carson herself died of cancer in 1964.) Following the publication of *Silent Spring*, Robbins helped develop the Breeding Bird Survey, a continent-wide census of birds designed to track changes in populations. "Rachel was right about the drastic effect DDT was having on populations of birds, fish,

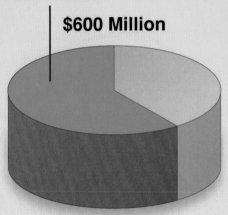

Estimated Funds Needed over Five Years (2007–2012) for Clinical Development of Malaria Vaccine

Up to 60 percent will go toward clinical vaccine trials in Africa.

$600 Million

Taken from: *Science Daily*, "Malaria Research Booming, but Scientific and Technical Gaps Apparent, Report Shows," October 8, 2007.

and other wildlife," Robbins says. "The peregrine falcon and the brown pelican, in particular, were rapidly heading for extinction, and hundreds of other species were showing drastic declines."

A Danger to Birds, but Not Necessarily to Humans

In fact, Carson may have underestimated the impact of DDT on birds, says Michael Fry, an avian toxicologist and director of the American Bird Conservancy's pesticides and birds program. She was not aware that DDT—or rather its metabolite, DDE—causes eggshell thinning because the data were not published until the late 1960s and early 1970s. It was eggshell thinning that devastated fish-eating birds and birds of prey, says Fry, and this effect is well documented in a report on DDT published in 2002 by the Department of Health and Human Services' Agency for Toxic Substances and Disease Registry (ATSDR). The report, which cites over 1,000 references, also describes how DDT and its breakdown products accumulate in the tissues of animals high up on terrestrial and aquatic food chains—a process that induced reproductive and neurological defects in birds and fish.

FAST FACT

The Stockholm Convention in Persistent Organic Pollutants is an international treaty to restrict and eventually end the use of dangerous synthetic chemical pesticides, including DDT. As of February 2009, 162 countries were parties to the convention; the United States was not among them.

On the subject of cancer, however, the evidence is more equivocal. Although the EPA [Environmental Protection Agency] has classified DDT and its metabolites, DDE and DDD, as "probable human carcinogens," and although mice exposed to DDT for more than a year did develop liver tumors, a detailed analysis of multiple studies of breast, pancreatic, prostate, testicular, and other forms of cancer in people led the authors of the ATSDR report to conclude that "there is no clear evidence that exposure to DDT/DDE causes cancer in humans."

So is it safe to apply DDT to combat malaria? One advocate for its use is Donald Roberts, a medical zoologist recently retired from the Uniformed Services University of the Health Sciences in Bethesda, Maryland, and a member of the board of Africa Fighting Malaria, which collaborates with conservative think tanks. "The reason that I promote the use of DDT is because, number one, it's very cheap," he says. "Number two, it's long lasting. And number three, as a repellent it keeps mosquitoes from entering the houses to a greater degree than any other chemical that we know of." Roberts has studied malaria transmission in Central and South America for three decades and claims that spraying DDT inside houses—while avoiding its use in agriculture—has already produced "spectacular declines" in malaria rates in those regions.

Ambiguity over Effectiveness Against Malaria

But elsewhere, the picture is murkier. According to the World Health Organization (WHO), over 500 million cases of malaria occur each year, resulting in an estimated 1 million deaths. Most of these cases of illness and mortality occur in sub-Saharan Africa. But no one can say whether malaria rates have increased or declined in Africa as a whole in recent decades because of difficulties in collecting data, says Valentina Buj, public-health officer for the WHO's Global Malaria Programme in Geneva. Some countries do not track whether DDT has been used to combat malaria. "Given the wide variation in the transmission of the disease—endemic areas, areas of low endemicity, hyperendemic areas, and sometimes these strata all occurring in the same country—we prefer to look at each country separately without aggregates over the entire continent," Buj says.

The confusion is also reflected by the fact that in the past year [late 2006 to late 2007] officials at the WHO have issued contradictory directives on the use of DDT to fight malaria. On September 15, 2006, Arata Kochi, the head of the Global Malaria Programme, announced at a news conference in Washington, D.C., that DDT posed no health risk when sprayed in small quantities on the inside walls of houses, and he called for an expansion of its use to combat the mosquito-borne disease. Then on May 3, 2007, Maria Neira, director of the WHO's public-health and environment department, said at a Dakar, Senegal, meeting of the ratifiers of the Stockholm Convention—an international treaty that went into effect in 2004 that controls the use of persistent organic pollutants like DDT—that the WHO's goal was to reduce the use of DDT and eventually eliminate it.

Lost in all the hullabaloo is the fact that DDT has never been completely banned for use in public-health measures. The Stockholm Convention defines disease control as an "acceptable use" for DDT, and 13 countries in Africa and Asia have registered their intention to use it as such. Among them is South Africa, which claims significant success in controlling malaria since DDT was reintroduced to that country in 2000. According to South Africa's department of health, the number of malaria cases in the country dropped by 65 percent between 2005 and 2007, and deaths from the disease fell by 73 percent. The agency attributes the decline to an increase in indoor spraying with DDT, but also to earlier surveillance and detection of the illness in malaria-prone regions and the use of a drug, artemisinin, to treat multidrug-resistant strains of the malaria parasite.

Danger of Resistance

Given the fact that DDT does appear to be effective at fending off malaria mosquitoes in some places, its use would seem logical—but if applications do become more widespread, users may encounter a problem that Carson herself highlighted in *Silent Spring:* resistance to the insecticide by the Anopheles mosquitoes that transmit malaria, says Michael Fry. Since *Silent Spring*'s publication, hundreds of mosquito species have become resistant to DDT, and although the rise of resistance has slowed since the ban on the agricultural use of DDT, many mosquito populations are already immune to its effects, says Pierre Guillet, of vector control and prevention at the WHO's Global Malaria Programme. While the main malaria vector in South Africa, *Anopheles funestus*, is susceptible to DDT, a secondary vector, *A. arabiensis*, has developed resistance to DDT and other insecticides. Elsewhere in Africa, mosquito resistance to DDT is already common. "DDT resistance in Africa as well as several other parts of the world has been acquired because of massive use of these insecticides for crop protection," Guillet says.

That's why Fry and others believe that a broader and better solution is one that would help humans while

A Kenyan farmer inspects his Artemisia plant crop. When the drug artemisinin, extracted from the plants' leaves, was used in conjunction with DDT spraying over a two-year period, malaria cases in South Africa were reduced by 65 percent and deaths by 73 percent. (Jack Barker/Alamy)

minimizing the impact on wildlife and the environment. That solution is a suite of techniques called integrated vector management: draining mosquito-breeding pools, spraying safer, less persistent pesticides known as permethrins, and plastering homes with mosquito-repelling lime. This last approach has been applied successfully in Mexico, which no longer uses DDT for vector control. "No single pesticide will ever solve the problem," Fry says. "What you need to do is use a variety of different pesticides in different years to minimize the insect resistance problem. You want to use other techniques as well—wetlands management, netting, screens, repellent chemicals indoors. If you rely on a single chemical like DDT, you're going to fail."

Bed Nets Should Be Distributed to the Poor Free of Charge

Awash Teklehaimanot, Jeffrey D. Sachs, and Chris Curtis

While everyone agrees that insecticidal-treated bed nets are one of the most effective means of lowering malaria infection rates, profound disagreement exists over what is the best way to get the bed nets to those who need them. In the following selection economist Jeffrey Sachs of the Columbia University Earth Institute and his associates Awash Teklehaimanot and Chris Curtis contend that free universal distribution of the nets is the most simple and effective means of combating malaria. Sachs, Teklehaimanot, and Curtis argue that social marketing of nets—wherein bed nets are sold at low costs in malaria-endemic regions—cannot reach those in the most remote areas, and even deeply discounted bed nets are beyond the reach of the poorest people, most of whom live on less than one dollar a day.

SOURCE: Awash Teklehaimanot, Jeffrey D. Sachs, and Chris Curtis, "Malarial Control Needs Mass Distribution of Insecticidal Bednets," *Lancet*, vol. 369, June 21, 2007, pp. 2143–46. Copyright © 2007 Elsevier Limited. All rights reserved. Reproduced by permission.

L ong-lasting insecticidal bednets (LLINs) are one of the major ways to control malaria, and they are widely accepted worldwide by communities in areas affected by malaria.[1,2] One LLIN costs about US$5 to manufacture and is effective for about 5 years. They have two kinds of protective effects—one for the people directly under the nets, and one for the community at large. The second effect is important, but often ignored. By achieving high community coverage to ensure a substantial community protection, malaria-control efforts can be more powerful than when only individual protection is attempted.

The direct effect of LLINs is to protect the people sleeping under them, and it operates in three ways. First, the insecticide kills some of the *Anopheles* mosquitoes after a few minutes. Second, the LLIN repels a proportion of the mosquitoes after contact.[3] Third, the net acts as a mechanical barrier to biting. The mechanical barrier provides half or less of the protection, which is why bednets without insecticide are less effective than treated ones. A torn and untreated net offers little or no protection, but a torn pyrethroid-treated net still works well.[4] LLINs provide good protection at only about $1 per net per year, with an average of around 1.7 people using every net.[5,6] The result is remarkable low-cost protection against disability and death, notably for people who are most vulnerable, including infants, small children, and pregnant women.

Insecticidal nets provide good, but not perfect, protection for users,[7] but the community effect[6,8–10] can extend the protection beyond that for the individuals under the nets. By greatly reducing malaria transmission, LLINs decrease the risk of others in the community coming into contact with an infected mosquito. Every LLIN user thereby contributes not only to his or her safety, but also to the safety of others—the mass effect. The effect is analogous to herd immunity from vaccines. To have

A Zimbabwean woman puts her child inside an insecticide-impregnated mosquito net. Such nets serve as a barrier against mosquitoes, killing some and repelling others. **(Philinon Bulawayo/Reuters/ Lando)**

maximum effect within communities, LLIN coverage should be as high as possible, with a target of complete coverage.

The mass effect works in three ways. First, mass coverage by LLINs reduces the number of mosquitoes in the community.[6,8–10] Second, mass coverage shortens the lifespan of the mosquitoes,[8] thus reducing the possibility for maturation of *Plasmodium* sporozoites and hence decreasing the proportion of mosquitoes that become infective.[6,8–10] Therefore the possibility of transmitting the illness to others is greatly reduced. Third, with some *Anopheles* species, mass coverage might divert mosquitoes from human to animal biting, thereby reducing human-to-human transmission. However, *A gambiae* is so anthropophilic [human-loving] that, even with nearly 100% coverage with insecticidal nets, about 80% of blood meals were found to come from human beings.[8] Taken together these effects on the vector population can greatly reduce transmission of disease,[11,12] but only if the coverage of mosquito nets is sufficiently high. Importantly, at low coverage, the mosquitoes that are deflected by the nets will tend to seek out another human being to bite. There would be little or no reduction in overall transmission, but only a diversion. If transmission was diverted from high-risk to low-risk individuals, that would be beneficial but there would be no major effect on intensity of transmission of malaria in the community.

Optimum community protection is achieved when mass coverage with LLINs is combined with universal access for the community to timely and effective treatment in the event of infection. Timely treatment can also be expected to have a community benefit. By clearing the infection in the patient as soon as possible, the individual is not only cured of the disease but is also no longer a reservoir of parasites for transmission to others. Therefore LLINs and timely treatment with appropriate medicines (eg, artemisinin-based combinations) should be seen as a package for protection of the individual and reduction of transmission in the community.

In devising bednet policies, many donor agencies aim to protect only the vulnerable groups rather than the entire community, and as a result do not achieve the full potential of the method to restrict or stop transmission of the disease. This is a false economy. First, the donors miss the chance to reduce malaria transmission if they narrow the protection against the disease. Second, and crucially, the donors' definition of vulnerable is too narrow. The donors seek to protect children younger than 5 years and women who are pregnant, on the grounds that malaria is especially likely to kill individuals in these two groups. Yet children older than 5 years and adults other than pregnant women are also vulnerable to severe illness, death, and substantial economic costs from the disease.

These risks will probably increase as climate change and population movements bring malaria epidemics to new regions and unprotected populations, in which children older than 5 years and adults have not acquired partial immunity. Even when adults do not die of the disease, they can become ill, at high economic and social cost to the community because malaria is especially common at seasons when labour is greatly needed for planting and harvesting.[13] Whole communities of adult workers at harvest time are often beset by illness that results in food insecurity all year round.

Moreover, links between malaria and AIDS emphasise the dangers of assuming that adults are not vulnerable groups. Malaria infection can raise the viral load of individuals infected with HIV, thereby increasing the probability of transmission of HIV through sexual contact. Malaria infection, in other words, might well be a cofactor in transmission of AIDS. Thus malaria control should also provide some protection against HIV-transmission.[14,15] Because malaria is a cofactor in many types of infectious diseases, its control will have many protective effects on health that extend beyond the direct effects on malaria itself.

The full value of LLINs in personal protection and reduced malaria transmission will therefore depend on high rates of LLIN coverage, combined with effective and timely management of malaria infections when they arise. For a typical household of five people, there will be three sleeping sites that need bednet coverage, so that each net on average will protect about 1.7 individuals. The yearly costs of protection are therefore minimal—about $0.60 per person per year.

Present coverage in Africa with insecticide-treated bednets remains low with, in many places, 10% or fewer people being provided for. However, in a small but growing number of countries, campaigns of mass distribution of bednets are now being supported by the International Red Cross, the Global Fund against AIDS, Tuberculosis and Malaria, and other partners. Until these recent mass-distribution campaigns, the usual donor strategy has been social marketing of bednets and insecticides, with subsidies to vulnerable groups. Social marketing of bednets has not been a success, and coverage has remained low, especially in rural areas where malaria transmission is far more intense than it is in urban areas.[16] This strategy has led to low and slow uptake of nets and insecticides[17–20] and sales have been limited to the narrowly defined vulnerable groups, and to individuals who can afford to pay. The aim has generally been to sell bednets to vulnerable groups at what donors regard as low cost—eg, $1–2 per net, which are sold to pregnant mothers at antenatal clinics. Yet even this low cost is too high for tens of millions of households, especially in rural areas, with little cash income and with restricted access to formal health services (where the nets are marketed).[17–21] Intensive marketing efforts have often taken 5 or more years to reach even a third of the vulnerable population. Many human and financial resources have been devoted by donor agencies to such efforts. Large amounts of money are spent on advertising and promotion of the nets, rather than on the nets themselves.

> **FAST FACT**
>
> A 2007 study of insecticide-treated bed net use in Kenya found that when bed nets were sold commercially in 2004, only 7 percent of children slept under nets. By the end of the first year of free distribution in 2006, two-thirds of children were sleeping under treated bed nets.

Education of poor communities to properly use LLINs and artemisinin-based combinations is a good strategy, but unless awareness is coupled with free availability of the essential commodities, the outcome is futile—knowledge will not serve these communities if they do not have access to these commodities because of poverty. Poor people cannot afford the nets[17–21] or the drugs, and the present marketing approach has left most of Africa at risk.

Free mass-distribution of LLINs—with the highest priority given to rural areas where malaria transmission is most intense, but aiming to cover all regions of malaria transmission—can work most effectively if the distribution is not only to especially vulnerable individuals but to all sleeping sites in every household. Successful mass-distribution campaigns have occurred in several countries, led by the International Red Cross or by national efforts supported financially by the Global Fund and other partners.[22] Ethiopia offers an important example.

Ethiopia needs around 20 million nets for 34 million residents in malaria-transmission areas. Between 1990 and 2004, donor agencies obliged Ethiopia to sell the bednets to achieve partial cost recovery. About 1.5 million nets were imported to the country over 10 years under the cost-recovery scheme, and national net coverage was low. With a new commitment by the health authorities in favour of mass distribution of free nets, backed by the Global Fund, a striking increase in bednet distribution and coverage has been achieved since 2004.

2005 saw the importation and distribution of 4.3 million nets, rising to 7.4 million in 2006 and another 6.7 million nets in 2007 being procured, for a total of 18.4 million nets in 3 years. This substantial effort at free distribution has had many supporters, including the Global Fund, UNICEF, World Bank, Department for International Development (UK), Canadian International Development Agency, Japanese International Cooperation

Insecticide-Treated Bed Net Distribution in Seven African Countries

Country	Insecticide-Treated Bed Nets Distributed as of 2008
Benin	1,700,000
Madagascar	1,500,000
Mali	2,262,404
Mozambique	698,000
Rwanda	1,350,000
Uganda	2,300,000
Zambia	500,000

Taken from: President's Malaria Initiative, "Progress Through Partnerships: Saving Lives in Africa. Second Annual Report," March 2008.

Agency, and the Carter Center (USA). Because of such goodwill and co-operative spirit of international agencies and the donor community, almost complete net-coverage in the malarious areas has been feasible in a short time. Yet although the success stories in Ethiopia, Niger, Togo, Sao Tomé and Principe, and some other countries with mass distribution are exciting, the shocking truth is that major donor agencies have continued to promote social marketing, despite its clear inadequacy. They also continue to support a narrow definition of vulnerable groups, thereby leaving most of the society vulnerable to malaria and failing to reduce malaria transmission through the mass effect.

Tragically, funds mobilised for malaria prevention and control are not used for saving lives, but are instead diverted to try to create new markets for bednets that do not exist. This approach has compromised the effectiveness of malaria control efforts. We strongly suggest that malaria-endemic countries and donor agencies should abandon the idea of social marketing, especially in rural areas greatly affected by malaria, and also in urban areas with malaria transmission. They should also commit to a policy that regards antimalarial commodities—such as drugs, diagnostic methods, and insecticides—as public goods to be available free of charge for mass distribution to affected communities. Comprehensive malaria control in Africa is achievable by 2010, at the minimal cost of $3 billion per year if sound principles of public health and economics are observed.[5,18,23] Millions of lives can be saved, and Africa will be given vital help in escaping from the vicious circle of poverty and disease that continues to grip the continent.

Notes

1. Lengeler C. Insecticide-treated bed nets and curtains for preventing malaria. *Cochrane Database Syst Rev* 2004; **2**: CD000363.
2. Binka, FN, Kubaje A, Adjuik M, et al. Impact of permethrin impregnated bednets on child mortality in Kassena-Nankana district, Ghana: a randomized controlled trial. *Trop Med Int Hlth* 1996; **1**: 147–54.
3. Maxwell CA, Chambo W, Mwaimu, Magogo F, Carneiro IA, Curtis CF. Variation in malaria transmission and morbidity with altitude in Tanzania and with introduction of alphacypermethrine treated nets. *Malar J* 2003; **2**: 28.
4. Curtis CF, Myamba J, Wilkes, TJ. Comparison of different insecticides and fabrics for anti-mosquito bednets and curtains. *Med Vet Entomol* 1996; **10**:1–11.
5. Teklehaimanot A, McCord GC, Sachs J. Scaling up malaria control in Africa: an economic and epidemiological assessment. *AM J Trop Med Hyg* (in press).
6. Curtis CF, Maxwell CA, Finch RJ, Njunwa KJ. A comparison of use of a pyrethroid either for house spraying or for bednet treatment against malaria vectors. *Trop Med Int Hlth* 1998; **3**: 619–31.

7. Sormekun S, Maxwell CA, Zuwakuu M, Chen C, Michael E, Curtis CF. Measuring the efficiency of using treated bednets: the use of DNA fingerprinting to increase the accuracy of personal protection estimates in Tanzania. *Trop Med Int Hlth* 2004; **9:** 664–72.

8. Magesa SM, Wilkes TJ, Mnzava AEP, et al. Trial of pyrethroid impregnated bednets in an area of Tanzania holendemic for malaria: effects on the malaria vector population. *Acto Trop* 1991; **49:** 84–96.

9. Howard SC, Omumbo J, Nevill C, Some ES, Donnelly CA, Snow RW. Evidence for a mass community effect of insecticide-treated bednets on the incidence of malaria on the Kenyan coast. *Trans R Soc Trop Med Hyg* 2000; **94:** 357–60.

10. Hawley WA, Phillips-Howard PA, ter Kuile FO, et al. Community-wide effects of permetrin-treated bed nets on child mortality and malaria morbidity in western Kenya. *AMJ Trop Med Hyg* 2003; **68:** (supp 4): 121–27.

11. Le Menach A, Takala S, McKenzie FE, et al. An elaborated feeding cycle model for reductions in vectorial capacity of night-biting mosquitoes by insecticide-treated nets. *Malar J* 2007; **b:** 10.

12. Smith DL, McKenzie FE. Statics and dynamics of malaria infection in Anopheles mosquitoes. *Malar J* 2004; **3:** 13.

13. Working Group on Malaria. Coming to grips with malaria in the new millennium 2005. http://www.unmilleniumproject.org/reports/tf_malaria.htm (accessed June 21, 2007).

14. Wabwire-Mangen F, Shiff CJ, Vlahov D, et al. Immunological effects of HIV-1 infection on the humoral response to malaria in an African population. *AMJ Trop Med Hyg* 1989; **41:** 504–11.

15. Whitworth JAG, Hewitt KA. Effect of malaria on HIV-1 progression and transmission. *Lancet* 2005; **365:** 196–97.

16. Hay S, Guerra CA, Tatem AJ, Atkinson PM, Snow RW. Urbanization, malaria transmission and disease burden in Africa. *Nat Rev Microbiol* 2005; **3**: 81–90.

17. Snow RW, McCabe E., Mbogo CN, et al. The effect of delivery mechanisms on the uptake of bed net re-impregnation in Kilifi District, Kenya. *Health Policy Plan* 1999; **12**: 18–25.

18. Cham MK, Olaleye B, D'Alessandro U, et al. The impact of charging for insecticide on the Gambian National Impregnated Bednet Programme. *Health Policy Plan* 1997; **12**: 240–47.

19. Maxwell, CA, Rwegoshora RT, Magesa SM, Curtis CF. Comparison of coverage with insecticide-treated nets in a Tanzanian town and villages where nets and insecticide are either marketed or provided free of charge. *Malar J* 2006; **5**: 44.

20. Curtis C, Maxwell C, Lemnge M, et al. Scaling-up coverage with insecticide-treated nets against malaria in Africa: who should pay? *Lancet Infect Dis* 2003; **3**: 304–07.

21. Guyatt HL, Ochola SA, Snow, RW. Too poor to pay: charging for insecticide-treated bednets in highland Kenya. *Trop Med Int Hlth* 2002; **7**: 846–50.

22. Grabowsky M, Nobiya T, Ahun M, et al. Distributing insecticide-treated bednets during measles vaccination: a low-cost means of achieving high and equitable coverage. *Bull World Health Organ* 2005; **83**: 195–2001.

23. Sachs JD. Achieving the Millennium Development Goals—the case of malaria. *N Engl J Med* 2005; **352**: 115–17.

Bed Nets and Antimalaria Medications Should Be Distributed to the Poor at a Subsidized Cost

UNICEF

Mosquito nets and antimalaria medications are an essential part of malaria prevention, especially in Africa, where malaria kills a child every thirty seconds. Although many well-intentioned people believe distributing these provisions for free is the best way to protect the public from malaria, The United Nations Children's Fund, or UNICEF, has an antimalaria program in Malawi which provides bed nets and antimalaria tablets at a subsidized cost. This program has proven most effective. Distributing bed nets and antimalaria medications for a cost, even to the poorest of families, ensures that those that buy the supplies consider them valuable items. Also, even by selling the nets at a subsidized rate, UNICEF receives a profit, which enables the program to continue. The United Nations Children's Fund works for children's rights and their survival, development, and protection, guided by the Convention on the Rights of the Child.

In a small district hospital of Kasungu, central Malawi, Kate is wrapping her three-day-old son in a yellow blanket. She smiles at her baby, oblivious to her environment. She doesn't notice the green mosquito net

SOURCE: UNICEF, "Social Marketing Enables Widespread Mosquito Net Usage in Malawi," www.unicef.org, 2009. Reproduced by permission.

Malaria Cases in Rwanda, Africa, 2006

Malaria is notoriously difficult to track, with official cases accounting only for those that are reported. Millions more are likely.

Estimates Vary Widely

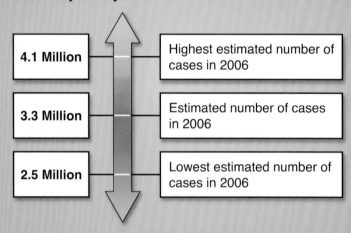

4.1 Million	Highest estimated number of cases in 2006
3.3 Million	Estimated number of cases in 2006
2.5 Million	Lowest estimated number of cases in 2006

Taken from: William Easterly, "Did Bill and Melinda Gates Claim Malaria Victory Based on Phony Numbers?" Aid Watch, February 11, 2009.

that hangs above her bed, like a colourful detail in the white room. This detail could save her son's life.

Malaria kills an African child every 30 seconds. A simple US$3 mosquito net could protect them from this deadly disease. Additionally, providing pregnant women with anti-malaria tablets twice during their pregnancy greatly reduces their risk of infection and of having low-birth weight babies, a major cause of infant death.

Mosquito Nets Are an Essential Part of Malaria Prevention

"I have had malaria and everybody I know has had malaria," says Kate. "During my pregnancy I came several times to the hospital for ante-natal [prenatal] check ups and the staff told me about mosquito nets. I will buy a net

PERSPECTIVES ON DISEASES AND DISORDERS

from the hospital when I go home. I want to protect my baby." She also received an anti-malarial drug during the fourth and seventh months of her pregnancy.

Kate is one of the 2,500 women who delivered their infant at the Kasungu hospital in 2002 and bought a mosquito net for 50 kwacha (less than 20 US cents). The price of the mosquito net, which is sold with an insecticide treatment kit, is heavily subsidized by UNICEF in the rural hospitals and health care centres of Malawi, one of the poorest countries in the world. During the rainy season, when the risk of malaria is the highest, the Kasungu hospital sells up to 450 nets a day.

UNICEF, in collaboration with national and international partners, supports anti-malaria programmes focusing on children under the age of five and pregnant women in all sub-Saharan countries. In 2002 alone, UNICEF provided over 4.4 million mosquito nets to 25 African countries, for a total value of $9.5 million, making it the largest mosquito net buyer in the world. This represents a 175 per cent increase since 2001. In addition, UNICEF purchased $3 million worth of insecticide, used to treat the mosquito nets.

Malawi's Anti-malaria Programme Is Threefold

Pregnant women and children under five in rural areas can buy nets and insecticide for 50 kwacha (20 US cents). Pregnant women are also given anti-malaria tablets during their pregnancy and can buy the re-treatment kit (which includes an insecticide tablet, plastic gloves and a measuring plastic bag) for 20 kwacha (8 US cents).

Other rural families can buy the same nets for 100 kwacha (40 US cents) through their village health committees.

Urban families, which are better off, can buy the nets and insecticide at the commercial rate of 395 kwacha (US $4). Nets are not given for free, even to the poorest families, to ensure that they consider the net a valuable item. Communities themselves were consulted on the cost of the mosquito nets and agreed on the price of 50 kwacha. However small, this money contributes to the recovery of cost.

Selling Subsidized Nets Is Important

Nurses who sell nets receive a small incentive. Village health committees who sell mosquito nets receive 20 per cent of the price and can use this money for health-related activities in the village. In a village near Kasungu, the community was able to provide electricity to the local health facility. Another village drilled three wells to provide drinking water. In some cases, the Village Health Committee will receive a chicken or some maize flour in exchange for a net.

"We bought 120 mosquito nets in November 2001. We sold all of them and tomorrow I'll buy another 70 nets," says the chairman of the Kanin'ga village health committee in Kasungu district. "People have already paid for them. Some of our committee members were trained on the use and treatment of nets with insecticide, so that they can inform families who buy them."

Both at the hospital and at the village level, women who buy mosquito nets receive information about the proper use of the net and its re-treatment. This information supplements the simple colourful leaflet that accompanies the net and the treatment kit. In urban centres, mosquito nets are available in many shops. It is not rare to spot a net between a pile of eggs and soft drinks. The nets are blue and conical, and the packaging is more sophisticated and also contains the same re-treatment kit. Signs promoting the use of mosquito nets dangle outside the shops.

FAST FACT

UNICEF, in collaboration with national and international partners, supports antimalaria programs focusing on children under the age of five and pregnant women in all sub-Saharan countries. In 2002 alone, UNICEF provided over 4.4 million mosquito nets in 25 African countries, for a total value of $9.5 million, making it the largest mosquito net buyer in the world.

The commercial sale of mosquito nets became national in November 2002, and over 136,000 nets were sold in just one month. "Since the actual cost of an insecticide-treated net is about US$3, commercial nets are sold with a profit. This profit helps covering the cost of subsidized nets. It's important for the sustainability of the programme", explains Dr. Desmond Chavasse, the Director of Population Services International (PSI) in Malawi.

This strategy, called social marketing, is being used in many countries to increase the use of mosquito nets and other health-related items. It focuses on the urban middle and upper class families who can afford to buy a mosquito net at a commercial price. "This way, we ensure that our limited resources are used for the poorest and most vulnerable populations: pregnant women and children under five in rural villages," says Dr. Chavasse.

A worker applies disinfectant to mosquito netting in a Tanzanian textile plant. (Jim Young/ Reuters/Landov)

Malaria Is One of Many Diseases That Will Resurge with Climate Change

World Health Organization

The World Health Organization reports in the following viewpoint that many transmissible diseases are at risk of resurging due to climate change, including dengue fever, diarrhea, and malaria. In the case of malaria, evidence from the African highlands in the east suggests that incidence of the disease is already increasing, which coincides with a warming trend in the region over the past thirty years. Malaria is not typically associated with high altitudes and latitudes, and it tends to be particularly virulent in warm, humid conditions. As infectious diseases spread to new regions, so does the danger that appropriate health services will not be available and that populations will have no immunity, which will put a huge stress on health care systems. The World Health Organization is an arm of the United Nations that deals with international health issues.

SOURCE: *Protecting Health from Climate Change, World Health Day 2008*, 1211 Geneva 27, Switzerland: World Health Organization, 2008. Copyright © World Health Organization (WHO). Reproduced by permission.

Infections caused by pathogens that are transmitted by insect vectors are strongly affected by climatic conditions such as temperature, rainfall and humidity. These diseases include some of the most important current killers: malaria, dengue and other infections carried by insect vectors, and diarrhoea, transmitted mainly through contaminated water.

Malaria Distributions Are Strongly Affected by Climate

Transmitted by *Anopheles* mosquitoes, malaria is the most important vector-borne cause of mortality globally. It kills almost 1 million people each year, mainly poor children in Africa. Malaria is strongly influenced by climatic conditions; it is not transmitted in the cooler temperatures associated with high altitudes and latitudes, and the number of mosquito vectors depends on the availability of freshwater breeding sites. Warmer temperatures, higher humidity and more places where water can collect generally favour malaria transmission. There is evidence that in some sites in the highlands of East Africa, a warming trend over the last 30 years has improved conditions for mosquitoes, increasing the probability of malaria transmission and highland epidemics.

Dengue Prevalence Is Expanding Rapidly

Transmitted by *Aedes* mosquitoes, dengue is a fast growing challenge, particularly in tropical cities in developing countries. Cases have risen dramatically in the last 40 years, as unplanned urbanization with standing water in waste and other receptacles have created mosquito breeding sites, and movement of people and goods has spread both mosquito vectors and

FAST FACT

"Disease vector" is a term that refers to an organism that carries a disease-causing pathogen—a virus, a bacterium, or, in the case of malaria, a parasite—but does not actually cause the disease. In the transmission of malaria, mosquitoes are the only known vector.

infections. For the same reasons, the distribution of dengue is also highly dependent on climate. In the absence of changes in other determinants, studies suggest that climate change could expose an additional 2 billion people to dengue transmission by the 2080s.

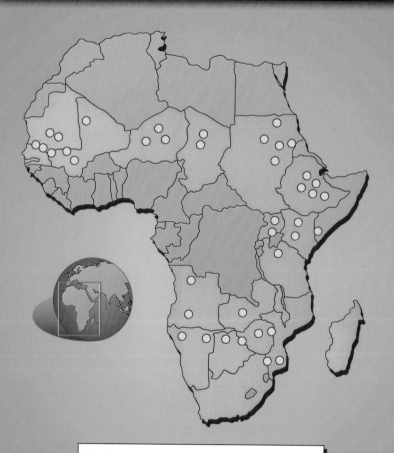

Malaria Epidemics in Africa, 1997–2002

○ Documented malaria epidemics

Taken from: World Health Organization, "Coming to Grips with Malaria in the New Millennium," United Nations Development Programme, 2005.

To prevent an outbreak of dengue fever, a worker in Paraguay fumigates an area where mosquitoes typically breed. (Jorge Adorno/Reuters/Landov)

Diarrhoea Remains One of the Biggest Killers of Children

Viruses and bacteria transmitted through water and contaminated food can cause severe diarrhoea in children, often locking them into a vicious cycle of undernourishment, susceptibility to other infectious diseases, and eventually death. Higher temperatures and too much or too little water can all facilitate transmission of this disease. In countries with inadequate water and sanitation services, diarrhoea is much more common when temperatures are high. For example, rates of diarrhoeal disease in Lima, Peru, are 3–4 times higher in the summer than in the winter, increasing by 8% for every 1°C increase in temperature. Both flooding and unusually low levels of water can also lead to water contamination and bring higher rates of illness and death from diarrhoea. Warming and greater variability in precipitation threaten to increase the burden of this disease.

Many Other Diseases Will Also Be Affected

Any disease caused, transmitted or harboured by insects, snails and other cold-blooded animals can be affected by a changing climate. For example, climate change is projected to widen significantly the area of China where schistosomiasis transmission occurs. Together, vector-borne diseases kill over 1.1 million people and cause the loss of 49 million years of healthy life, every year. Effects on infectious disease will not be restricted to developing tropical regions. For example, climate change is also expected to change distributions of diseases such as Lyme disease and tick-borne encephalitis, and to increase rates of *Salmonella* and other foodborne infections in Europe and North America.

New and Unfamiliar Infections Strain Health Services and Economies

When infectious diseases appear in new locations, where people do not have immunity and health services may not have experience in controlling or treating infections, the effects can be dramatic.

Global Climate Change Will Not Influence the Incidence of Malaria

Paul Reiter

The history of malaria epidemics suggests that outbreaks of the disease are not limited to warm climates; in fact, the worst recorded epidemic occurred in the former Soviet Union in the 1920s, with as many as 13 million cases a year. Malaria persisted in Europe until the twentieth century, when a DDT spraying campaign virtually eliminated it. In sub-Saharan African countries, where malaria is endemic, malaria may be influenced by climate factors such as heavy rainfall, but this is not the only factor. More significant are pervasive poverty, lack of infrastructure, resistance to insecticides and antimalarial drugs, and deforestation, argues Paul Reiter in the following viewpoint. These factors typically are ignored by those who claim that global climate change will increase the worldwide incidence of malaria infection, including the United Nations–based Intergovernmental Panel on Climate Change. Reiter is chief of the Insects and Infectious Disease Unit at the Pasteur Institute in Paris, France. He has been a vocal critic of the Intergovernmental Panel on Climate Change.

SOURCE: Paul Reiter, "Malaria in the Debate on Climate Change and Mosquito-Borne Disease," United States Senate Committee on Commerce, Science, and Transportation, April 26, 2006. Reproduced by permission of the author.

I am a specialist in the natural history and biology of mosquitoes, the epidemiology of the diseases they transmit, and strategies for their control. I worked for 22 years for the Centers for Disease Control and Prevention (CDC), including two years as a Research Scholar at Harvard. I am a member of the World Health Organization Expert Advisory Committee on Vector Biology and Control. I have directed many investigations of outbreaks of mosquito-borne disease, and of others such as Ebola Haemorrhagic Fever. I was a Lead Author of the U.S. National Assessment of the Potential Consequences of Climate Variability and Change. I am presently Professor of Medical Entomology at the Institut Pasteur in Paris, France.

In this brief presentation I restrict my comments to malaria, and emphasise four points:

1. Malaria is not an exclusively tropical disease.
2. The transmission dynamics of the disease are complex; the interplay of climate, ecology, mosquito biology, mosquito behavior and many other factors defies simplistic analysis.
3. It is facile [overly simplistic] to attribute current resurgence of the disease to climate change, or to use models based on temperature to "predict" future prevalence.
4. Environmental activists use the "big talk" of science to create a simple but false paradigm. Malaria specialists who protest this are generally ignored, or labelled as "sceptics."

In the early 1990s, malaria topped the list of dangerous impacts of global warming; the disease would move to temperate regions as temperatures increased. This prediction ignored the fact that malaria was once an important cause of morbidity and mortality throughout most of the US and Europe, even in a period that climatologists call the "Little Ice Age." In the US, as in western

Europe, prevalence declined in the 19th century as a result of multiple changes in agriculture and lifestyle that affected the abundance of mosquitoes, their contact with people, and the availability of anti-malarial drugs. Nevertheless, the most catastrophic epidemic on record anywhere in the world occurred in the Soviet Union in the 1920s, with a peak incidence of 13 million cases per year, and 600,000 deaths. Transmission was high in many parts of Siberia, and there were 30,000 cases and 10,000 deaths in Archangel, close to the Arctic circle. The disease persisted in many parts of Europe until the advent of DDT. Clearly, temperature was not a limiting factor in its distribution or prevalence.

Malaria Activists Changed Focus

In the mid-1990s, activist emphasis changed to transmission in poorer countries, often referred to as those "least able to protect themselves," particularly in sub-Saharan Africa. Yet in most of the continent, temperatures are far above the minimum required for transmission, and most of sub-Saharan Africa, transmission is termed "stable" because people are exposed to many infective bites, sometimes more than 300 per year, so annual incidence is fairly constant. Mortality is highest in "newcomers"—young children and immigrants. Those that survive acquire a partial immunity that reduces the risk of fatal illness. In other regions, transmission is endemic but "unstable" because annual transmission is variable; the potential for epidemics is great because immunity declines in periods of low transmission. Climatic factors, particularly rainfall, are sometimes—but by no means always—relevant.

In recent years, activist emphasis has shifted to "highland malaria," particularly in East Africa. Despite carefully researched articles by malaria specialists, there has

> **FAST FACT**
>
> The Intergovernmental Panel on Climate Change was formed in 1988 by the World Meteorological Organization and the United Nations Environment Programme to act as a clearinghouse for scientific research on global climate change.

Costs of Malaria Preventives and Treatments in Sub-Saharan Africa, in U.S. 2003 Dollars

Intervention	Annual per Capita Cost	Total Annual Cost (in millions)
Insecticide-treated bed nets	$8.12 per child	$496
Intermittent preventive treatment	$2.02 per pregnancy	$10
Changing to artemisinin-based combination therapy (ACT)	$0.83 per malaria case	$140
Scaling up ACT use	$5.66	$177
Total		**$824**

Taken from: World Health Organization, "Coming to Grips with Malaria in the New Millennium," United Nations Development Programme, 2005.

been a flurry of articles by non-specialists who claim a recent increase in the altitude of malaria transmission attributable to warming, and quote models that "predict" further increase in the next 50 years. Tellingly, they rarely quote the specialists who challenge them. Nor do they mention that maximum altitudes for transmission in the period 1880–1945 were 500–1500m *higher* than in the areas that are quoted as examples. Moreover, highland above 2000m constitutes a mere 1.3% of the whole continent, an area about the size of Poland that is totally dwarfed by regions of stable and unstable transmission at lower altitudes.

Politics Versus Science

A galling aspect of the debate is that this spurious "science" is endorsed in the public forum by influential panels of "experts." I refer particularly to the Intergovernmental Panel on Climate Change (IPCC). Every five years, this UN-based organization publishes a "consensus of the world's top scientists" on all aspects of climate change. Quite apart from the dubious process by which these scientists are selected, such consensus is the stuff of politics, not of science. Science proceeds by observation, hypothesis and experiment. The complexity of this process, and the uncertainties involved, are a major obstacle to meaningful understanding of scientific issues by non-scientists. In reality, a genuine concern for mankind and the environment demands the inquiry, accuracy and scepticism that are intrinsic to authentic science. A public that is unaware of this is vulnerable to abuse.

Felled trees litter a Sierra Leone mountainside. Deforestation, as well as poverty, lack of infrastructure, and resistance to anti-malarial drugs, make malaria difficult to control in sub-Saharan Africa. (**Chris Jackson/ Getty Images**)

The current increase in malaria is alarming, but the principal factors involved are deforestation, new agricultural practices, population increase, urbanization, poverty, civil conflict, war, AIDS, resistance to anti-malarials, and resistance to insecticides, not climate. In my opinion, we should give priority to a creative and organized effort to stem the burgeoning tragedy of uncontrolled malaria, rather than worrying about the weather.

The Effects of Global Warming on Diseases Such as Malaria Are Still Unclear

Maria Said

When a village in Italy was struck with the tropical disease chikungunya in the summer of 2007, scientists were puzzled and wondered if the outbreak had been caused by climate change. With outbreaks of cholera, diarrhea, and contagious gastrointestinal illnesses already on the rise and associated with the rising water temperatures of El Niño, many researchers believe a warming climate may lead to the resurgence of malaria in regions where it was eradicated in the mid-twentieth century, including Europe and the United States. Other scientists are skeptical, though, arguing that the Italian chikungunya outbreak was actually caused by a genetic mutation in the virus, while others maintain that it was the result of increased international travel and globalization. Maria Said maintains in the following viewpoint that, ultimately, predicting the movement of infectious diseases across regions is nearly impossible, and proving that such movement is caused directly by climate change is equally unlikely. Nonetheless, many in the scientific community are unwilling to take chances, contending that factors such as poverty, crowded and inadequate housing, and a lack of infrastructure ultimately will make certain areas more vulnerable to epidemics regardless of weather. Said is a fellow in the infectious diseases unit at Johns Hopkins Hospital.

SOURCE: Maria Said, "The Chikungunya Effect: What Effect Does Climate Change Have on the Spread of Disease?" *Slate,* February 6, 2008. Reprinted with permission.

Before the summer of 2007, Castiglione di Cervia, Italy, was known as a quiet village near Ravenna. In July, however, doctors noticed complaints of excruciating joint pain, fever, headaches, and rash. Their patients were experiencing a fever called "chikungunya"; the word originates in the Makonde language in Tanzania and Mozambique and means "to dry up or become contorted." This epidemic had two years previously raged unexpectedly through islands in the Indian Ocean. But it was new to Europe.

And so Castiglione found itself at the center of scientists' efforts to map the effect of climate change on the spread of infectious disease. In December, at a Washington, D.C., conference sponsored by the Institute of Medicine [IOM], scientists and doctors wrestled with these questions: Did global warming bring chikungunya to Italy? Will it lead to a return of scourges like malaria, pushed out of Europe and the United States in the mid-20th century? Will epidemics worsen in poorer countries?

Already, there are suggestions of change. Rising water temperatures off the coast of Alaska allowed the bacteria *Vibrio parahaemolyticus* to move much farther north than previously, contributing to a 2004 outbreak of gastroenteritis in cruise ship passengers from contaminated oysters. Higher temperatures in Peru during the 1997–1998 El Niño phenomenon were associated with a doubling of diarrhea cases requiring hospital admission in children. Earlier in the 1990s, El Niño–associated coastal temperature changes off Peru cultivated an unusual abundance of plankton and are believed to have contributed to an unexpected cholera epidemic affecting nearly 1 million people and killing almost 8,000 in Latin America.

Scientists Dispute Effects of Climate Change on Disease

While they readily accept the associations between climate and infectious agents, scientists balk at stating exact-

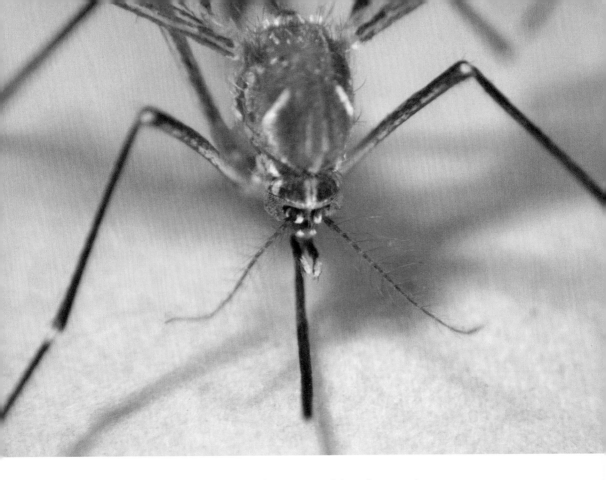

ly what a change in climate might cause. This reluctance lies both in the complexity of disease and in the nature of science, in the need to build a case incrementally, fact by fact. Asking a scientist to predict the spread of disease is like asking him or her, while standing in the midst of a tornado, to predict how the landscape will change by measuring the direction and amount of debris flying by.

Take the chikungunya debate: Initially hailed as a clear example of how warmer weather can lead to new epidemics, some experts pointed out that it was not global warming but a new mutation of the virus that made the fever increasingly infectious. Others argued that the reasons for the chikungunya epidemic lay in new routes for disease opened up by the global economy; in the 1990s, imported tires carried into Italy a mosquito known as "the Asian tiger," which can serve as a vector for chikungunya as well as dengue fever.

The Asian tiger mosquito can serve as a carrier for both the chikungunya virus and dengue fever. (**Mark Fairhurst/ Photoshot/Landov**)

The association of malaria epidemics with warmer temperatures in the Ethiopian highlands proves equally difficult to pin down. Many factors other than temperature play a role in transmission. Paul Reiter, a medical entomologist at the Pasteur Institute in France, names several: forest clearance, wetlands drainage, agricultural fertilizers, herbicides, stagnant water, people's daily activity patterns, the location of homes in relation to mosquito breeding sites, the designs and materials of those homes, the presence or absence of screens and bed nets, chemotherapy, vaccination, and mosquito control. Can we extricate climate change from such a web?

Multiple Factors Affect Disease

There is no way to conduct the kind of experiment— one group of people exposed, another similar group not exposed—that would more definitively establish the effect of climate change on the spread of a given disease. To make things more complicated, climate and the other factors that affect diseases interact with each other. What if increasing temperatures cause people to stay in their homes and thus actually prevent disease transmission? What if drought causes people to wash their hands less and spread bacteria more? What if floods in Asia cause chaotic mass migrations and further disease spread?

Scientists also use mathematical formulas and, increasingly, computer models to try to predict the future. But because of the number of variables a computer model would have to account for, it would seem that unless God was your statistician, you would be hard pressed to "prove" that climate change X will cause disease Y. At the IOM conference, Michael Osterholm, director of the Center for Infectious Disease Research and Policy, voiced his frustration with these limitations in demonstrating cause and

FAST FACT

Severe malaria outbreaks in the Punjab region of India in the early twentieth century have been definitively linked with excessively high rainfall and humidity during the monsoon season.

effect. "We are struggling to prove it with scientific data, and we can't," he said. "We don't need West Nile virus to know we are in deep doo-doo. . . . [I]f we are trying to solve it on individual studies, we will be in the court of science for a long, long time, and then it will be too late."

Theoretical Acceptance of the Cause

What is the alternative to endless discussion? Recent editorials in the *New England Journal of Medicine* and the *Lancet* call for accepting, even without 100 percent certainty, the accumulating body of evidence that climate change will affect infectious diseases. Doctors regularly make recommendations to patients based on what they

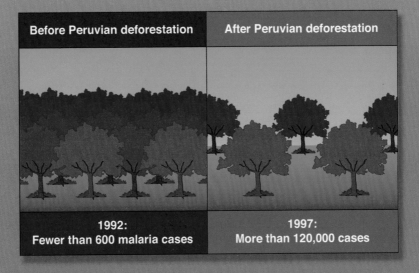

Deforestation Increases Rates of Malaria

A study in the Peruvian Amazon showed that malaria-inducing mosquitoes bite humans about 200 times more often in areas where forests have been cleared to make way for crops or towns (deforestation) than in forested areas.

Before Peruvian deforestation	After Peruvian deforestation
1992: Fewer than 600 malaria cases	1997: More than 120,000 cases

Taken from: Paroma Basu, "As Amazon's Tree Line Recedes, Malaria-Wielding Mosquitoes Buzz In," *University of Wisconsin–Madison News*, January 3, 2006.

think might happen. Gina Solomon, a physician and senior scientist for the Natural Resources Defense Council, points out that not knowing whether hypertension will hurt an individual patient does not stop a doctor from trying to bring his or her blood pressure down.

A different slant, put forth by Peter Schwartz and others at the consulting agency Global Business Network, sidesteps the need for scientific proof. Their "systems vulnerability approach" does not try to predict what will happen to the climate; rather, it identifies existing vulnerabilities in our world that could easily tip a region toward a new epidemic given the additional stress of climate change. A damaged Iraqi town without a clean water source is more vulnerable to a cholera outbreak if waters there warm, as they did in Peru. An unusually hot summer in a sprawling slum in Mexico City becomes the breeding ground for an epidemic of infectious diarrhea. We may not know precisely what causes what. But we don't have to sit back and wait to see what the weather will do.

CHAPTER 3

The Personal Side of Malaria

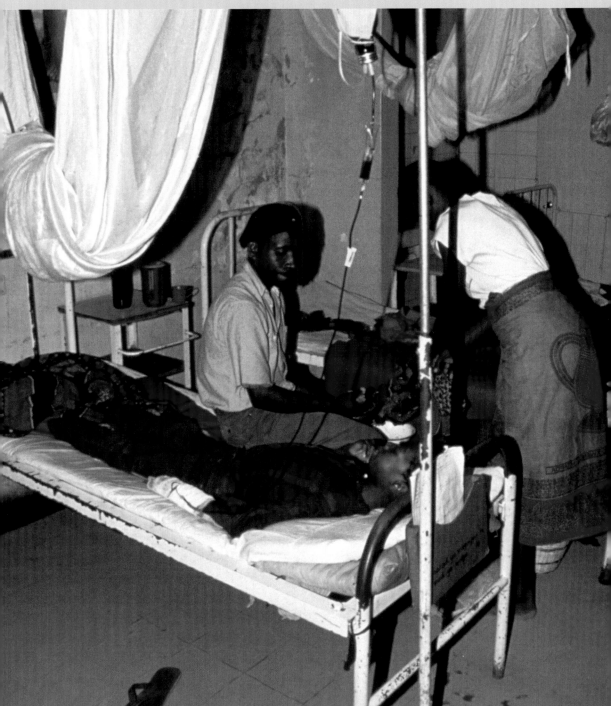

Lack of Money Is the Most Common Issue Prohibiting Parents from Treating Their Children

Mark Dlugash

Women in the Acholi Quarter, a slum in Kampala, Uganda, typically earn less than one dollar per day, many by working in stone quarries or selling vegetables, beads, or other wares. Malaria is a daily threat, with most children contracting the illness numerous times every year. Author Mark Dlugash reports that this puts enormous financial strain on families already living in extreme poverty. Families fall deeper into poverty when parents, who themselves may have health problems related to repeated malaria infections, must stop working to care for sick or dying children caught in the constant cycle of infection. Children who have had numerous bouts of malaria frequently suffer from neurological problems and chronic weakness, making them unable to attend school and thereby exacerbating the cycle of poverty. Dlugash was an undergraduate student in psychology and education at Swarthmore College when he cofounded a group to raise awareness about malaria and encourage bed net use in Uganda.

Photo on previous page. A young boy in a Tanzanian hospital receives a blood transfusion to treat his malaria. (Andy Crump/TDR/World Health Organization/Photo Researchers, Inc.)

I was in Uganda with Katie Camillus helping her work on the establishment of a micro-loan enterprise for her work as a Lang Scholar. I asked one of the wom-

SOURCE: Mark Dlugash, "Interviews with Families Affected by Malaria," *Daily Gazette* (Swarthmore, PA), November 6, 2007. Reproduced by permission of the author.

en who had been helping us, Aciro Santina, if there were children with malaria in the Acholi Quarter, and she said there were very many. She arranged to let me interview kids with malaria and their mothers.

I soon realized that there was little sense trying to interview the kids, because they were listless and most of them did not have the energy to talk. In fact, I began to feel extremely guilty for even asking the parents to bring their children with them. I asked the mothers a set of basic questions: name, were they married, how many kids did they have and their ages and names, tell me about their kid with malaria, how did you know the kid had malaria, what did you do for treatment, how much did treatment cost, how much money do you make per month, what is your occupation, how do you feel when your child gets malaria, do you use bednets, why or why not (almost everyone said they'd like to but it costs way too much money), etc.

We did not advertise that we would pay mothers for the interviews, but we wanted to compensate them for their time, so all participants were paid 2000 Ugandan shillings ($1.25). I felt guilty that this is such a small sum of money, but it is about twice as much as most women make in a day. The women came without any expectation of payment, but rather because I was a guest in their community: they were showing me the hospitality and kindness to visitors which is customary in the Acholi culture. . . .

A Deadly Cycle of Illness

I started out by asking how many times their children had had malaria, and I soon found that the inevitable response was, "This year?" Most of the children had contracted malaria so frequently that the disease was just a fact of life. Even if mothers could afford the treatment, the children continue to contract malaria again and again because they do not have a way to prevent the disease.

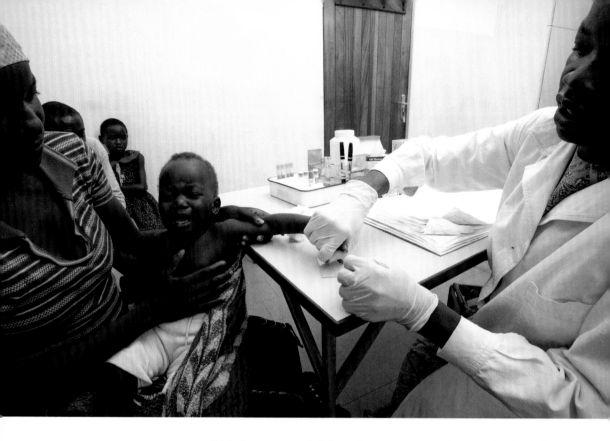

A Ugandan child has a blood sample taken to determine whether he has malaria. The prevalence of poverty in Africa means that few parents can afford preventive medical care. (**Mauro Fermariello/ Photo Researchers, Inc.**)

Life for many children becomes a cycle in which children get malaria, their parents do their best to scrounge up the money necessary for treatment, the children get better, and a few weeks or a month later, the children have malaria again. After this cycle happens too many times, the parents do not have any more money to pay for treatment.

Insecticide-treated bednets kill the mosquitoes that carry malaria and have the capacity to dramatically reduce malaria transmission. Unfortunately, at $10 per net, they are too expensive for all but the most well-off families: many of these women live on less than $1 a day. Again and again, mothers told me during their interviews that they would love to have bednets for their children, but they simply cannot afford them. . . .

Eunice with Her Son Oroma

They are originally from Kitgum in the North and were displaced during the war; Oroma has had malaria 3 times.

PERSPECTIVES ON DISEASES AND DISORDERS

Eunice knows he has malaria because after the temperature is very high, she goes to the clinic and they check the blood. Now he is coughing, and hasn't talked since he got malaria.

The treatment costs 20,000–60,000 Ugandan shillings ($15–$45), and Eunice makes 20,000 Ugandan shillings ($15) a week selling tomatoes—so malaria pills cost her half a month's salary. She can't afford to go back for more malaria pills because there is no more money.

She says: "It is not okay. When there is sickness you cannot feel okay. You become very worried. If it increases he will pass away. You just become very worried."

Akello Pasqua and Amono Samuel

Akello has nine kids at the ages of 21, 18, 16, 14, 12, 10, 8, 5, and 3, three of whom currently have malaria. At the beginning of this sickness he [Samuel] was not moving at all—he has been sick for two weeks. It is the 5th time he has been admitted to the clinic with malaria, though he has been sick many more times. She says, "I don't have money to take the boy to the hospital. Samuel is sick again and there is no money for treatment."

The clinic gave them quinine and syrup for 7,000 Ugandan shillings ($5), but they did not have enough money to pay. Akello Pasqua sells paper beads to raise money to take [her] son to the clinic; the family does not have bednets.

Santina Aciro and Isaac

Santina is an orphan, and her parents and grandparents are dead. Santina also has a 6 year old and a 1 year old—Amito and Teddy. Isaac has had malaria three times, but a quinine injection would cost between 5,000 and 30,000 Ugandan shillings (between $4 and $23).

She says, "He'd start vomiting. His body would become so hot, even the eyes—start crying. I feel so bad. The condition is bad. The temperature is so high. The body is so hot. I want to have a bednet, but I do not have the money to buy it. 30,000 ($23) is the most I make in a month. But even the rent is 15,000 ($12.50) per month. If I did not have enough money, I would go to the stone quarry. But I am not going. I have chest pain. I don't have money."

Stella Amollo's Family

Stella is a loan officer, so she makes 80,000 ($60) per month—an extremely high wage in the Acholi Quarter. Before the micro-loan enterprise came, she worked in the stone quarry crushing stones and made 30,000 ($23) a month—less than a dollar a day. She strongly disliked working in the stone quarry.

Marcy had malaria in June, was really sick, vomiting, could not eat, missed school for one week and could not study. Prisqua had malaria in June 2007, and has had malaria over 20 times per year. In June, she recovered after 4 injections which cost 12,000 ($8). Marcy recovered also after one week—had malaria treatment (10,000) and typhoid (30,000)—cost 40,000 ($30) total to treat.

Stella says, "I feel sad. I cannot be happy when she is sick. How can I feel better when she has not yet recovered? I need to get money, I need to take her to the hospital. I do not even have time to cook for these ones who are remaining. It stops me from working, even my personal work on paper beads, because I need to take care of them in the hospital."

Amal Cecilia and Oren Simon

Amal Cecilia has 8 children. She is not working. Her husband died, and she is supported by his army pension monthly salary of 240,000 per month ($180—very high for this community). Oren is very sick and cannot eat. He's been vomiting yellow, and he's had malaria more than 20 times. Treatment costs 50,000 ($38) at the hospital, and the younger kids do not have bednets.

Obtaining Antimalarial Medication

In 2007 more people in Ugandan provinces obtained antimalarials from private-sector organizations than from any other source.

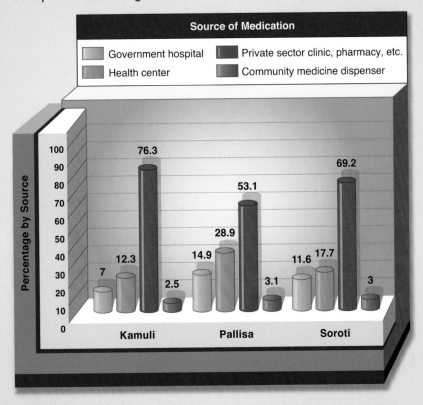

Source of Medication

- Government hospital
- Health center
- Private sector clinic, pharmacy, etc.
- Community medicine dispenser

Percentage by Source

Kamuli: 7, 12.3, 76.3, 2.5
Pallisa: 14.9, 28.9, 53.1, 3.1
Soroti: 11.6, 17.7, 69.2, 3

Taken from: Medicines for Malaria Venture Annual Report 2007. www.wmv.org/IMG/pdf/mmvAR.07_Lrez_All.pdf.

Amal Cecilia says, "When the sickness comes, he can't even talk. He loses consciousness. Everyone thinks he is going to die. He starts feeling headache, then throwing up. Most times it comes suddenly when I do not have money, and I am not able to pay at once. The nurse knows me and allows me to pay in installments. I would like to have a bednet. There are so many things to pay for: the little money I get goes to school fees. I am the only one taking care of him—he has no father and there is so much to pay for. I feel pain. I feel so bad. They call suddenly, 'Simon is sick.' I feel such pain. It is always him. I pray to God."

Margaret and Children

Margaret has 6 children. Emmanuel has had malaria seriously 4 times; Loy has had it over 20 times. Her husband works in the quarry, and so does she. She makes about $1 a day (1500–2000) and 45,000–60,000 a month total (up to $45)—combined, she and her husband make about $1.25 a day. Effect of quinine—child has diarrhea and vomits, then she feels better for a short time, then they fall sick again within two weeks.

> **FAST FACT**
>
> Two of the longest-used treatments for malarial fever are derived from plants. Artemisinin comes from the herb sweet wormwood, and quinine is derived from South American cinchona bark.

Margaret says, "Whenever they fall sick, the temperature gets high. The girl begins convulsing. I have to keep putting cold water on them. With the boy, if I don't take him to the hospital immediately, the treatment is more expensive. Most times I am not able to pay. I try to pay in installments. I plead with them. Then I go to the quarry. I work, I get a little money, I buy the medication. I can't pay when I don't have the money. I must use the money that I would use for eating. What can I do? Sometimes when the children fall sick I give them quinine tablets—it can help a little, but they get sicker until they get injections at the hospital. There is no money to buy the bednet. If I had the money then I would use them. When the children are sick, I feel sick. I become sick myself."

Akello Helen and Irene

Irene has had malaria over 20 times. Akello Helen has had 8 children, and two of them died of malaria, so now she has 6. Her husband is a builder—he earns about 30,000 ($23) a month, but the rent costs 50,000 ($37.50) a month. When her kids fall sick, they usually have malaria. Now Irene feels very dizzy when she is moving.

She says, "Irene cannot go two months without falling sick. When I give Irene tablets, she throws up. I pay in installments to the doctor until I can get the rest of the money. So many times, there is no money to take the child to the doctor. The child is sick now, but there is no money to take her to the clinic.

"I feel so bad. It comes when I don't have the money. The only way to save her is to take her to the clinic. I really feel pain. I feel frustrated. I pray to God that God should help the child because there is no money and I am powerless.

"I have a lot of problems. I am sick. I cannot do the hard work in the quarry. I have no source of income. I have chest problems. Some of the children are not studying because I have no money to pay for them. I am looking after two orphans. The orphans are not studying because I have no money to pay for them."

Abalo Christine and Teresa

Teresa recently had malaria, and she has had malaria more than ten times. Christine works for an HIV/AIDS organization and takes care of 2 orphans from her deceased brother, who was killed in the war in the north. She has 5 children, all of whom have had malaria.

Christine makes 110,000 ($83) a month and $1000 per year—but school for her oldest child alone costs 900,000 per year ($675).

She says, "When Teresa has malaria, she doesn't want to breastfeed. The temperature is high. I rush her to the clinic. They test the blood for the parasite. We don't have a good clinic here. Sometimes, when you don't have money, you run to the neighbor. If the neighbor doesn't have money, the child doesn't get treatment. We have lost very many children here to malaria . . . malaria is very common. You find it in each and every family. If my child is sick, I also feel sick. I can't even eat."

A Philanthropist Explains That Eradicating Malaria Will Take Investment and Innovation

Bill Gates, interviewed by Kristi Heim

The Bill & Melinda Gates Foundation began its work in malaria eradication with a $50 million grant in 2001. Since then the disease has burgeoned, particularly in sub-Saharan Africa, and resistance to conventional treatments has increased, most notably in Asian countries. Moreover, the remoteness of the disease from the everyday lives of most Westerners makes interest in a long-term awareness campaign difficult to sustain. On the other hand, in malaria-endemic regions people have a high level of understanding about the causes and prevention of malaria, so reaching those populations with preventive measures and, eventually, a vaccine, promises to be effective. But the most pressing issue in malaria research is resource allocation, with, according to Gates, most spending on infectious disease research currently going toward the least problematic disease burdens, largely because those illnesses threaten the wealthiest countries. Gates maintains that this inequity is the greatest obstacle to eradicating malaria. Bill Gates is a cofounder of the Microsoft Corporation and the Bill & Melinda Gates Foundation, a philanthropic organization that devotes a large portion of its focus to malaria research. Heim is a writer for *The Seattle Times*.

SOURCE: Kristi Heim, "A Q&A with Bill Gates," *Seattle Times*, September 25, 2007. Reproduced by permission.

Kristi Heim: How was it that malaria first caught your attention?

Bill Gates: Well, malaria's one of the biggest killers in the world. It was in the United States in a very serious way, but not during my lifetime. The Centers for Disease Control [and Prevention] started out as the malaria war control board based in Atlanta. Partly because the head of Coke had some people out to his plantation and they got infected with malaria, and partly [because] all the military recruits were coming down and having a higher fatality rate from malaria while training than in the field. We wiped out *Anopheles* [the mosquito that carries the malaria parasite] with the help of DDT.

Heim: Was there something that convinced you to become fixated on solving the problem of malaria?

Gates: Well, malaria is a terrible disease and when you talk to people who've had malaria, you get a sense of how horrific that is. It's terrible for everybody, but it's most severe for infants who are very weak and often die of cerebral effects, and pregnant women.

So there's a burden of malaria in terms of miscarriage and low birth weight that is actually hard to tally up. You might die of diarrhea or pneumonia, but it all goes back to that low birth weight that was [caused by] your mother's malarial episode. It's a horrific thing. And actually the disease burden even beyond the million a year killed, you've got all the people who have the disease.

My experience of malaria was just taking anti-malarials, which give you strange dreams because I don't want to get malaria. And then just looking at the numbers and seeing how unbelievable it is that it's gotten so little attention.

We announced a $50 million grant a long time ago. It would have been like 2001. And that doubled the private giving to malaria work, which seemed totally strange at a time when baldness or erectile dysfunction are getting huge $500 million budgets put into them.

This disease whose impact is easily a million times greater was getting almost nothing.

Actually malaria has killed more people. . . . It's setting a record every year. That is the number of people who died of malaria was higher last year [2006] than any year in history. Now it's not as widespread in the world [as it once was]. But the population growth in the areas where it's endemic, specifically Africa, has gone up enough, and you have difficulties in drug resistance and just lack of attention. That means it's worse.

In world health, everything's not worse. Measles certainly killed like 4 million a year and is now below a half-million a year. Polio was widespread. Now it's completely gone; no, almost gone. Smallpox is gone.

Malaria, if you take the top diseases other than AIDS, which has grown quite dramatically, and the TB [tuberculosis] piece that comes with that, malaria is one of the worst stories, and yet not that much has been put into it. AIDS you can say OK, because some small percentage of the infection was in the rich world there was a ton of money at least that went into drugs to treat it. In the case of malaria the lack of attention was completely across the board—vector control, drugs to treat and vaccines. All of those have a place to play. The vaccine is the high risk, high impact approach. If we had a perfect vaccine, many of the other efforts you wouldn't need. A vaccine's tough enough that we're working on them all in parallel.

Heim: At the launch of Windows Vista, you mentioned launching a malaria vaccine in the future. Americans are fairly self-absorbed. How can you get people excited about something that doesn't affect them?

Gates: Well, I think when smallpox was eliminated, the whole world got pretty excited about that because it's just such a dramatic success. And if we can finish polio, everybody will feel good about that, particularly organizations like Rotary or others who really played such a central role in it.

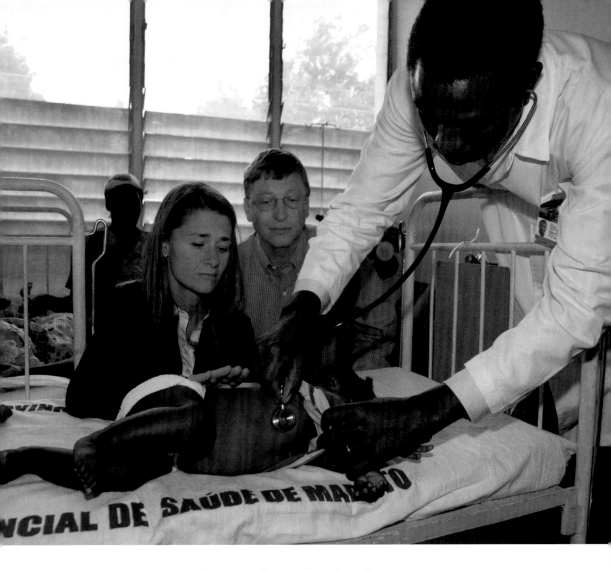

In the case of malaria, it does take place far away. Many speeches I've given, including the Harvard commencement speech, touch on the general theme of why don't we give more, why doesn't the richest country or the people in the richest country give more? The distance is a key thing. The fact that it's not part of our life experience.

If we re-sorted the world and your neighbors were dying of malaria—that a kid you'd met and had a human connection with—the amount of urgency, resources going into this would be a hundred times what it is even now. I mean it would be viewed as a total crisis. . . .

Bill and Melinda Gates visit a young malaria patient in Mozambique, Africa. The Gates Foundation contributed $50 million in 2001 to combat malaria worldwide. (**Jeff Christensen/Reuters/ Landov**)

Heim: The technical side of developing a vaccine is so complicated, but then so are the logistics of getting it out to people. What have you learned about that side of the equation?

Gates: A vaccine with a modest number of doses, often three, you can get lifelong immunity. The logistics of getting a malaria vaccine out . . . it's hard. But malaria is a very recognized disease. People are in deep fear [for] their child. When they start to get fever, they almost hope it's some respiratory thing because malaria can so quickly create the fever that disables or kills the child. Unless you can get in and get an IV with the right stuff there's a good chance your child may die. The demand side on this one, if we have the full impact, the demand will be very high. Amazingly vaccination can work even in places where there's not a lot of infrastructure. It's a lot easier to get vaccines out than it is to put someone on lifelong treatment for a disease like AIDS, so called anti-retroviral treatment, where you're looking for side effects and they've got to take their pills every day. Here we're talking about if we have a vaccine just getting them in childhood or maybe a booster as you get older. But that's way, way easier. Unlike some diseases like AIDS where the connection between what caused it, what made you sick. Here with malaria the understanding of the disease is very high amongst people who live in Africa, and there's no kind of denial or shame associated with this disease. It's all out in the open.

Now there are people who aren't as optimistic as me about the vaccine who say OK we need to take our current interventions and go after those. The foundation is part of that as well. The President's Malaria Initiative, the Global Fund money, some World Bank money, Nothing But Nets. If you compare that to even five years ago, there's a ton going on to take known interventions, including the nets and using the insecticides the right way. There's a thing the foundation was involved in inventing called intermittent treatment, where you don't actually prevent the episodes but because you have partial immunity you reduce the chance of them being fatal quite dramatically. Those are two new tools that I think are fantastic. The Zambia thing that we're one of the big movers in involves taking all these things and applying them. Melinda actually was in Zambia and saw those activities. I have not been there. Until after July 1, I don't get to visit any malaria sites, but I will after that.

Heim: You're making some very big bets. Do you ever worry that your motives will be misinterpreted or that you will be viewed as an outsider trying to impose your solutions onto others? Why should the world trust you?

Gates: Well, I don't think those issues really come up here. The strategy we're pursuing on malaria involves bringing together the top malaria people in the world. I wish there were more of them. Then they might even disagree more. But there's not that many malaria experts in the world. And so when [doctor] Regina [Rabinovich] goes to Johns Hopkins and London School and maybe about 20 other places and gathers 4 or 5 people from each place . . . you're talking about a very high percentage of people whose lives are devoted to malaria drug intervention, both vaccine and drugs and you could even throw even the insecticide group, which is a tiny little group. Have you ever heard of a new insecticide invented since DDT? No. Zero money went into that.

If we only had the money to fund drugs or vaccines, or if only to fund one drug or one vaccine, then we'd be making hard choices. Not me so much but Regina Rabinovich and people on her team . . . they're the experts on these things. We're backing all the things we can see that have a chance of success. It's lucky we have the resources to do, be able to do, that. If we hear of some new great thing we'll go and back that as well. It's not a field where there's a bunch of companies trying to do malaria that nobody knows about. This is a pretty small field. . . .

Heim: But since the world health community hasn't solved these problems you've been talking about, does it need a fresh approach? Are there some changes to the system that are needed?

Gates: Well the allocation of resources to go after infectious diseases—that needs to change. Remember we benefit from biological understanding, particularly of the immune system. The NIH [National Institutes of Health] spends $30 billion a year. . . . That's the platform we live on. . . . So every year the increased understanding helps us, helps our grantees.

FAST FACT

According to the World Health Organization, malaria infects half a billion people annually, 60 percent of them on the African continent, and kills a child every thirty seconds. And while insecticide-treated bed nets are known to be an effective preventive against the spread of the disease, only 3 percent of African children live in households with a bed net.

It's great the health community does research. The only thing that's strange is that when it goes beyond basic research to applied research, there's a huge tilt of the money going into things where there's rich world markets. That's to be expected, and you have to offset that by some degree of government grants and philanthropy to make sure that the diseases of the poorest don't get completely ignored. And they have been largely ignored. Ninety percent of the world's spending on infectious disease goes on 10 percent of the problems, and 10 percent of the money goes on 90 percent of the problems.

Look at the number of articles that were about SARS [severe acute respiratory syndrome] than about malaria, and then compare the disease burden. Well SARS, hey, there were some rich people. Some got sick and some almost got sick. That was different, new, scary, unbounded; whereas malaria, it's hey a million a year this year. 1.1 million next year. 1.2 million the next year. It just goes on and on. . . .

Heim: Many U.S. charities are motivated to help others by religion. But can secular people be just as driven to do good in the world? Tell me about your underlying motivation.

Gates: Well, the United States as a country believes in equity and that's a very tough thing to deliver, whether it's gender equity or racial equity.

But the biggest inequity is if you look globally and see the conditions that the poorest are condemned to, the way that, despite any motivation or ability on their part they can't put themselves into a reasonable situation. They can't get away from the disease and the lack of resources. Anyone who gets awareness of that, just on pure humanistic grounds or religious grounds, will really want to say, "Wow, why haven't we done better?"

Are we really going to look back and say that the world set its priorities properly?

We were involved in the commission that set up these Millennium Development Goals. That's been a great thing that articulates companies have a report card, students have a report card. Here's a world helping the people in need report card. Even if the world falls short, which on some of the goals it will, particularly related to Africa, the fact that it got the attention and drew people in to think about it, and think about innovative ideas for achieving those goals, it's been a fantastic thing overall.

The foundation is measuring itself by saving lives and improving these conditions. We think that's a very exciting thing to work on. Every philanthropy gets to pick their own things to work on: the ability to bring organizational approaches in, the ability to bring the latest science in, to draw on the smartest people. I saw that it was a pretty unique time for those pieces to come together, and then I saw the shocking vacuum that was there in terms of how little activity, either philanthropic or governmental, for the infectious diseases of the developing countries. I said OK, that's what we should go and do and just stay at it as long as it takes. . . .

Heim: What is it that you want to contribute most to conquering malaria in the end?

Gates: Well, to get the disease burden to be extremely low. If you can reduce the 200 million malaria episodes a year—a million deaths a year—the impact that has just in and of itself is mind blowing. . . . If you saved someone's life, you say, "Wow, that's big." If you saved 10, 100, 1,000, 10,000, if you go into those communities and see what it means to those mothers and fathers and how they spent their savings to go to the hospital to try to save the kid I'm just hopeful we can have a huge impact on this disease, by bringing the right people in, by using the latest biology, by getting a lot more money into it and tapping into some private-sector actors.

This is the time period where malaria can largely be conquered. And we'll just keep trying. We're five years into it and things, I'd say, have gone very well.

Mothers Take Extreme Measures to Save Their Children from Malaria

Amy Ellis

In Mali, families are organized around the husband's or father's leadership, and women usually must obtain permission from their husbands to get medical treatment for their children. In the following viewpoint author Amy Ellis reports on the case of a mother named Fatoumata, whose husband's denial of her request nearly cost their daughter her life when she developed severe malaria at age four. Sensing her daughter's tenuous hold on life, Fatoumata went to her brother-in-law for permission to take the girl to a health center. As the head of the entire household, the brother-in-law agreed to allow Fatoumata to take his niece for help, but he had no money to offer for payment. Fatoumata carried her daughter five miles until she reached the bus to take her to the village where her brother lived, and he gave her enough money to pay doctors at the medical center. By the time she reached the clinic, her daughter was suffering from severe anemia caused by malaria and needed a blood transfusion. Although Fatoumata's blood type was compatible, doctors at first refused to perform the procedure without her husband's permission. Knowing her child would die without the transfusion, Fatoumata convinced the technicians to do the transfusion anyway. Her daughter survived because of her tenacity, but Fatoumata has since suffered from weakness and fatigue due to the transfusion. Ellis is a writer for the Johns Hopkins School of Public Health's Voices for a Malaria-Free Future campaign.

SOURCE: Amy Ellis, "Malaria in Mali: A Mother's Perseverance," *Voices for a Malaria-Free Future,* 2007. Reproduced by permission.

The life of Fatoumata is characteristic of many women in Mali: She lives in a small, isolated village in the rural countryside and spends each day caring for her children, preparing meals for her family, working in the fields, searching for firewood, transporting water from the local well, washing clothes, and a multitude of other household chores. She has never been to school and was married at the age of eighteen. She is her husband's second wife and left her childhood village to reside with the extended family of her husband. Fatoumata is thirty-eight years old and has six children.

And not unlike many other Malian women, Fatoumata is a mother who would go to great lengths to ensure the health of her children. Although she may not realize it, Fatoumata's youngest child, a four-year-old daughter named Amina, is a testament to her mother's dedication and unfailing love. The child often fell ill with fevers, but they typically subsided within a few days. However, during one of these episodes, Amina's symptoms did not go away. At night, Amina's fever raged, causing the child to toss and cry throughout the night. During the day her fever would subside, but Amina was left exhausted, lethargic, and unable to eat.

Fatoumata attempted everything she could to alleviate her daughter's suffering, but Amina's condition seemed to only worsen. Fatoumata tried to quell her increasing panic and anxiety, but on the third day of the illness, she felt certain that her daughter's life was in danger. In three short days Amina's little body had become frail, feverish and pale.

"I saw the way in which her body changed," recounts Fatoumata. "She was closer to death than she was to life. I was terrified."

Defies Husband to Get Daughter Help

Knowing that time was crucial and that Amina was in dire need of medical care, Fatoumata turned to her husband for help, telling him that Amina was in danger of dying and needed to go to the health center as soon as possible. But despite her entreaties, Fatoumata's husband did not acknowledge her request and left to work in his millet field. By withholding a response, Fatoumata's husband could not be held responsible for denying her the ability to seek care, but by the same token, he provided neither the authorization nor the financial means necessary to obtain treatment.

Unwilling to accept his silence, Fatoumata followed him to his field. As her husband worked, Fatoumata walked behind him, begging him for help and warning him that failing to do so might result in the death of their daughter. Despite her determination, there was no reply.

"I thought that the child was going to die," said Fatoumata. "Normally, a father should take charge when there is an illness and be responsible for all of the costs. But sometimes, a mother is obligated to do the impossible to take care of her child."

> **FAST FACT**
>
> Severe anemia is common in malaria cases. When the *plasmodium* parasite enters the bloodstream via a bite from a mosquito, the *plasmodium* travels to the liver and begins to invade red blood cells to replicate itself. As the immune system tries to fight the infection, it attacks the red blood cells, causing their total number to drop.

Appeals to Brother-in-Law

So Fatoumata turned to her brother-in-law. Since he was the head of their entire household, she knew that her husband must answer his brother's request. Fatoumata explained Amina's dire situation and begged for help to take her to a health center. When questioned by his older brother, Fatoumata's husband finally responded that he had no money to give to Fatoumata for their child's care. Fatoumata's brother-in-law decided that although they were unable to contribute any financial help, Fatoumata was allowed to take Amina to a health center if she was able to find her own means to do so.

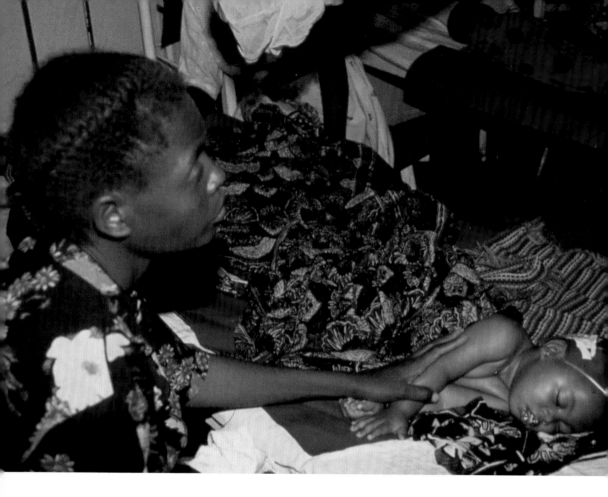

Mothers in Africa, like those the world over, will go to extraordinary lengths to save their children. (Andy Crump, TDR, World Health Organization/Photo Researchers, Inc.)

At four o'clock the next morning, Fatoumata carried Amina five miles to the nearest dirt road and waited for a vehicle traveling north toward the village where she grew up. Her own family was the last resort for financial help. Fatoumata arrived in her family's village late that afternoon and quickly sought out her younger brother, who willingly provided the funding necessary to pay for treatment. Fatoumata then raced Amina directly to the health center.

Upon seeing Amina's jaundiced eyes, pallid complexion and nearly lifeless state, the health agents quickly recognized that Amina had chronic malaria and was suffering from severe anemia. The child needed an immediate blood transfusion but there was no blood currently available. Fatoumata insisted that they check to see if her own blood was compatible, and if so, that they transfer her blood to her daughter.

PERSPECTIVES ON DISEASES AND DISORDERS

Negotiates with Health Care Agents

The health agents determined that Fatoumata's blood was compatible, but they could not do the procedure without the father's permission. Fatoumata knew that it was hopeless to wait for her husband, and she implored the agents to do the transfusion without him.

"I was afraid that my daughter was going to die even before we reached the hospital," Fatoumata said. "So when the agents said that I was going to be very tired when they took my blood, I told them it was okay, that they must cure my child at any cost. Regardless of the means, they must save my daughter."

Fatoumata's blood was transferred to her daughter and afterwards the child received medicine to treat her malaria. Fatoumata stayed with her family for a few days while Amina recovered before traveling back to her husband's village. In total, Amina's treatment cost twelve dollars.

Today, Amina's health is better, although she still suffers from occasional fevers. However, Fatoumata's own health has slowly deteriorated since then.

Suffers Efforts of Transfusion

"After they took my blood, the doctors told me to eat lots of meat, that I would become weak. But I don't have any money and I can't afford to eat meat. Now I am very feeble, I have headaches and often feel dizzy. But it was essential for me that my child be cured, even if I must die afterwards."

Despite the consequences of her blood transfusion, Fatoumata is grateful that her child was saved and now watches ever more vigilantly for signs of malaria in her children.

"Malaria is such a common illness among us," states Fatoumata. "Now, when I see that a child isn't improving after a day, I run quickly to the hospital. I don't play with childhood illnesses any more. Malaria is a very common illness among us, and chronic malaria is the worst of all."

Thankfully, because of her mother's resolve and sacrifice, Amina will not be one of the many children lost to chronic malaria.

Western Scientists Witness the Scourge of Malaria in African Countries

Rebekah Kent

While collecting research samples of malaria-causing *Anopheles* mosquitoes in southern Zambia, entomologist Rebekah Kent and her fellow researchers were stopped by the parents of a comatose three-year-old boy infected with malaria. The scientists agreed to drive the family to the nearest hospital, forty-five minutes away down dirt roads. In the following viewpoint Kent explains her fear for the child while also explaining the path of transmission from the delicate insects she carries in paper cups in her lap. Upon arrival at the hospital, they are told that the boy, named Frederick, is suffering from a lethal level of cerebral malaria. Days later, however, he has responded well to intravenous quinine and his prognosis is good. For researchers, however, he is only one of millions of children who are infected annually, three thousand of whom die every day. Kent is a postdoctoral investigator at the Centers for Disease Control and Prevention.

SOURCE: Rebekah Kent, "Saving Frederick: Entomologist Rebekah Kent's Tale of Death and Life at the End of Malaria Season," *Johns Hopkins Public Health,* Spring 2007. Reproduced by permission.

One morning last April [2006], I was riding shotgun in a truck in southern Zambia. Two Dixie cups of *Anopheles* mosquitoes in my hands and a dying boy in the back seat.

My colleagues and I had been in Mufwafwi village collecting mosquitoes as part of my dissertation research on the dynamics of malaria transmission. Complex and minute, anopheline mosquitoes are fascinating creatures. They also carry the malaria parasite that kills 1 million children each year in Africa alone.

As we were jovially piling into the truck to leave the village after a successful morning hunting "monzenyas," a man came running up to us with a limp child in his arms. A distraught woman followed close behind. Frederick looked about 3 years old and was completely comatose; only the whites of his eyes showed through partially cracked lids. None of us present was a physician, but the seriousness of his condition was clear. If he was going to have a chance of surviving, he needed a doctor as soon as possible. "Get in," we said. "Let's go."

Reaching a Hospital Is Difficult

April is the tail end of malaria season in southern Zambia. I'd seen many children sick with malaria in the Macha Mission Hospital, which is adjacent to the Johns Hopkins Malaria Research Institute's field station where my entomological research was based. Whether Frederick had malaria or some other infectious disease, we were clearly racing against time. Reaching the hospital is a big deal out there. We were a good 45-minute drive away, including 3 kilometers of bush paths before we would even get to the main road.

The mother held her sick child in the back seat. His breathing was raspy. I was terrified for him.

The truck bounced as quickly as safety permitted down eroded footpaths through tall grass. In my lap, I cradled the enemy. Topped by mesh held with rubber bands, each cup contained a dozen or so blood-laden anopheline mosquitoes that we had just collected. Some were from the very house in which little Frederick lived. With each bump the mosquitoes were jostled off their resting place on the side of the cup. Their threadlike hind legs arched up gracefully behind their bodies, and their fine, black and white dappled wings became gray blurs as they struggled to regain their footing. I tried to cushion them as much as possible.

Behind me, I heard Frederick alternate from uneven gasps to no sound at all. I gazed out the window and tried to concentrate on the pretty yellow and orange flowers that lined the roadside, on the bright sunlight that had just broken loose from an oppressive cloud cover. I caught a glimpse of the anguished father in the rearview mirror and clenched my jaw and swallowed hard to keep from crying. *Please*, let us get there in time.

Mosquitoes and Malaria Transmission

I looked back down at the mosquitoes in my lap and marveled that these tiny, delicate creatures could be the menaces responsible for some of the world's deadliest scourges. Any one of these mosquitoes I held in my hands could be harboring thousands of wriggling, microscopic parasites.

When a mosquito takes an infectious blood meal, the parasite burrows into the mosquito's midgut, where it encysts itself for about a week. Seemingly inert inside this oocyst, the parasite is rapidly multiplying into tens of thousands of minute infectious stage parasites called sporozoites. If the oocyst survives attack from the mosquito's immune defenses, it ruptures and releases the sporozoites into the mosquito's body cavity, where they penetrate the salivary

> **FAST FACT**
>
> Scientists estimate that 20 to 50 percent of the hundreds of millions of malaria infections that occur each year result in cerebral malaria, the most acute and deadly form of the disease, which occurs when infected red blood cells adhere to the vascular structures of the brain, blocking the flow of oxygen.

An electron microscope image shows an oocyst in the wall of a mosquito's stomach, from which tiny malaria sporozoites are bursting (upper right). The sporozoites will migrate to the salivary glands of the mosquito, which will infect the next human it feeds on. (**LSHTM/ Photo Researchers, Inc.**)

glands. From there, they are injected into a host upon the next blood feeding.

Mathematically, it is amazing that malaria transmission happens at all. Assuming the mosquito's very first blood meal was infected, she must live about 16 to 18 days in order to transmit the parasites. (Mosquitoes lucky enough to escape predation by birds, bats or raptorial insects may live about a month.) In the case of *Anopheles arabiensis*, the critical transmission time is the fourth or fifth blood meal. If this critical meal is taken on a cow, dog or chicken, the transmission cycle is broken. Likewise, if the first blood meal is taken from these animals or an uninfected person, the mosquito might not live long enough to become infectious. But, as Jeff Goldblum's character puts it in [the movie] *Jurassic Park*, "Nature will find a way." And nature had found its way into the back seat of our 4x4 Toyota Hilux.

Time Is Everything

Please, please, let us get there in time. The road seemed endless. I no longer heard breathing behind me.

Finally, we pulled into Macha and stopped at the hospital's front door. Later, Dr. Phil Thuma, a pediatrician and the executive director of the Malaria Institute at Macha, told us that Frederick had cerebral malaria and a +4 malaria smear—a lethal level. "I'm not sure he's going to make it," Thuma told us.

Over the next few days, Frederick responded well to intravenous quinine. He recovered, even managing to avoid the deafness and blindness often caused by cerebral malaria. To my relief and joy, the eyes that were once white slits gazed back at me, suffusing me in their deep brown, captivating warmth.

My happiness over Frederick's recovery was tempered, however, by my knowledge of malaria's grim reality in Africa. On that same April day that Frederick recovered, 3,000 other African children weren't as lucky. The malaria parasite found its way to them, and they died.

We just didn't get to them in time.

One Man's Belief in Modern Medicine to Treat Malaria Sets an Example for His Village

Voices for a Malaria-Free Future

Many people living in developing countries lack the money and access to information that allows them to treat malaria in the safest and most effective way. Too often this leads them to rely on outdated or traditional treatments. With some older malaria treatments, such as quinine and its derivatives, rapidly becoming obsolete because of growing resistance to them, obtaining the newer artemisinin-based combination therapy (ACT) is important to increase the chances of survival. Village healers also are of little use against malaria infection, but often, giving up old ways meets strong resistance. A father in Kalifabougou, Mali, maintained a belief in modern medicine because his older brother had become a medical doctor. When his own two-year-old daughter was infected with malaria, Zana at first purchased two older, less expensive treatments, hoping they would cure her. She began to recover, but it was short-lived, and two days later her fever increased and she had convulsions. Zana borrowed money on credit from neighbors in order to pay for the more current ACT treatment, which was successful. Voices for a Malaria-Free Future is a campaign run by the Johns Hopkins Bloomberg School of Public Health's Center for Communications Program.

SOURCE: "One Man's Belief in Medicine Sets Example for Whole Village," *Voices for a Malaria-Free Future*, 2007. Reproduced by permission.

In Mali, one of the poorest nations in the world, malaria is the primary cause of death among children under the age of five. Two million of Mali's young children have an average of two malaria attacks a year. Out of those two million children, 100,000 will have a severe attack with neurological complications or will die. With the increase in drug resistant malaria, the government, along with its global partners has changed the treatment protocols to a new combination therapy called artemisinin-based combination therapy or ACT. While ACTs are becoming more available in the local health clinics, poor families are challenged to make the right decision for a child who may be feverish when less expensive, but ineffective chloroquine or traditional healers are nearby as an option. Sometimes a whole village can benefit from the judgment and good decisions of one family.

The story of Zana illustrates this point.

As a young man, Zana moved to the rural village of Kalifabougou from a larger city in Mali where he spent his childhood years growing up. His older brother was a good student who went on to become a doctor and Zana adopted his brother's confidence in the usefulness and effectiveness of modern medicine.

In Kalifabougou, Zana lives with his wife and daughter. This is a village where many people rely on traditional therapies, but Zana believes that illnesses are best treated with modern therapies. "Modern medicine is fast and effective. It doesn't exhaust the mother and the child because it acts quickly," says Zana. "The main reason why people don't use modern medicine is because they lack money. If money is available, no one will say that they don't want to use modern medicine. When there is a vaccination campaign, women leave *en masse* with their children because it is free, but when they know they will have to pay a lot, they stay home. People love modern medicine, but it is poverty that keeps them from finding the right treatment."

Daughter's Fever Sparks Determination

Zana's belief was tested when his two-year-old daughter Fatim became sick with a fever. Worried that Fatim's fever was due to malaria, Zana took the extra money he made repairing motorcycles and used it to purchase chlorquine and paracetamol for his daughter. At first, the medicines seemed to help reduce Fatim's temperature, but the child vomited up part of the tablets and by the evening her fever intensified. "When her fever returned I thought the tablets were not sufficient to cure her so I decided Fatim needed to go to the health center right away," said Zana. There the health agents concurred that Fatim needed to be treated for malaria, and she was given several syrups and injections to cure her infection. Fatim responded favorably to the treatment and her parents took her home that night, hoping their daughter would soon fully recover.

Obsolete malaria treatments such as quinine have been replaced with artemisinin-based combination therapy (ACT), which combines newer antimalarial drugs with the traditional plant-derived drug artemisinin. (TH Foto-Werbung/Photo Researchers, Inc.)

Just two days later, when she was with her mother in a nearby village Fatim became feverish again. "It was so hard for my wife. She held Fatim to comfort her and after a few minutes Fatim's eyes rolled back in her head and she began to violently convulse," Zana explained. "My wife was shocked and terrified and hurried Fatim back to the health center in the village."

At the repair shop where he worked, word came quickly to Zana that Fatim needed additional treatment. But he knew, because of the cost of their recent visits, he did not have enough money left to pay for more medicines. Nonetheless, Zana recognized convulsions are a symptom of severe malaria and that his daughter absolutely required medical care. "There was no question I had to find a way to pay for Fatim's treatments," said Zana. He rushed over to a neighbor's house where he was able to borrow money on credit, and then raced back to the health center to meet his wife and daughter. Fatim was again treated for severe malaria, and after several injections and medications, her acute symptoms subsided. Zana followed his beliefs. And because of prompt medical attention sought by her parents, Fatim has since recovered and is now in good health.

Health Centers Are More Effective

Although many people are dissuaded from returning to the health center after one unsuccessful visit, Zana remains confident it is always the best way to treat illness. Zana reflects on his experience, "Two children might have the same illness, but one child might die because of a lack of money while the other might live because he received the right treatment. For example, my daughter had the same illness as another child in our village, but his par-

> **FAST FACT**
>
> Artemisinin-based combination therapy (ACT) is similar to combination therapies used to treat HIV/AIDS. ACT combines several antimalarial drugs with the traditional plant-derived treatment called artemisinin, which reduces the chances of the *plasmodium* parasite mutating to resist a single drug.

ents thought that he needed to be treated by a traditional healer. Sadly, now that child is dead, and thank God, my daughter is healthy." Zana's efforts have affected the lives of not only his own children, but hopefully have influenced the behavior of other parents in his village as well. "In our community, we men discuss health in general, and our personal experiences in particular, when we sit under the tree or where I work repairing motorcycles," Zana asserts. "I always tell my friends that if they have money, they should always take their child to the health center because it is faster and more effective. They should avoid neglecting an illness because then it will become severe and require more money and more effort." Both his words and his actions may help protect and save the lives of children in Mali.

GLOSSARY

anemia	A blood disorder common to malaria victims, especially infected pregnant women, characterized by a lack of the protein hemoglobin in red blood cells.
Anopheles mosquito	The genus of mosquito that most commonly transmits the malaria parasite to humans.
artemisinin	An antimalarial drug derived from the plant *Artemisia annua*, used to treat falciparum malaria, especially in regions where the disease has developed resistance to quinine.
artemisinin-based combination therapy (ACT)	The preferred drug treatment method, recommended by the World Health Organization to prevent increased resistance to antimalaria drugs, in which artemisinin is combined with other non-artemisinin-based drugs to treat the disease.
chloroquine	A drug used both to treat and to prevent malaria.
DDT	Dichlorodiphenyltrichloroethane, a controversial synthetic pesticide known to kill malaria-carrying mosquitoes but also to cause cancers and harm the environment.
indoor residual spraying (IRS)	A method of mosquito control wherein insecticides are sprayed on the interior walls of houses.
infectious disease	A disease that is caused by viruses, bacteria, fungi, protozoa, or parasites and transmitted among people or animals through bodily fluids, insect vectors, and contaminated air, food, liquids, or objects.

insecticide-treated nets (ITNs)	Netting material that has been treated with insecticides and is designed to be hung above a bed and draped over people in malaria-endemic regions while they sleep to protect them from mosquito bites.
Millennium Development Goals	Eight internationally agreed-upon target areas instituted by the United Nations Development Declaration to promote increased education, health, and economic status in underdeveloped nations, including the reversal of malaria incidence by 2015.
parasite	An organism that invades the body of another organism and lives off of it for a prolonged period of time.
Plasmodium falciparum	The most deadly species of malaria parasite.
protozoa	Single-celled microorganisms that may or may not be parasitic; *Plasmodium falciparum* is an example of a parasitic protozoan.
quinine	An antimalarial drug derived from the bark of the cinchona tree of Peru, first discovered to have antifever properties by the Quechua Indians and taken to Europe by Jesuits in the seventeenth century.
vector	An organism that carries and transmits infection but does not directly cause disease.

CHRONOLOGY

B.C.

Paleogene era The earliest known appearance of malaria-carrying mosquitoes, discovered frozen in amber dating back about 30 million years.

Paleolithic era Malaria is a threat to the earliest humans during the Stone Age.

Neolithic era Malaria infection influences the settlement patterns of humans as they evolve and begin settling in various regions around the world and developing agriculture about ten thousand years ago.

2700 One of the earliest written records of malaria infection appears in China.

ca. 500s Malaria symptoms are described in the Sanskrit medical treatise *Sushruta Samhita*, in which the disease is associated with biting insects.

ca. 400s The Greek physician Hippocrates relates malarial fever to seasonal changes and geographic location.

ca. 168 The herb *qinghaosu*, derived from the Artemisia plant, is first used as a remedy for malarial fever in China.

ca. 27 B.C.–A.D. 476 Epidemics of malaria may have a significant role in the fall of the Roman Empire.

A.D.

ca. 800–900 The term *mal'aria*, meaning "bad air," is coined in Italy, referring to the air in Rome's foul-smelling swamplands.

1095–ca. 1272 Malaria spreads throughout northern and western Europe when Christian crusaders bring the disease back from their religious battles in the Middle East and southern portions of Spain and France.

1500s Malaria appears in North America, most likely brought to the continent by European settlers and their African slaves. In South America, European explorers find that native Quechua Indians in Peru use bark from cinchona trees to treat fever.

ca. 1594–1623 William Shakespeare refers to malaria, long a scourge in England, in eight of his plays.

1607 Malaria ravages the Jamestown settlement, the first permanent English colony in North America, in what is now Virginia.

1632 A Jesuit missionary in Peru named Bernabé Cobo takes samples of cinchona bark back to Spain, where botanists and pharmacologists eventually refine the substance into quinine, which continues to be used as a malaria remedy.

1717 Italian physician and epidemiologist Giovanni Maria Lancisi relates malarial infection to the presence of flying insects in wetlands and recommends large-scale drainage of swamps.

1775 The American Continental Congress makes its first military expenditure, purchasing three hundred dollars' worth of quinine to treat malaria among the troops of General George Washington during the Revolutionary War.

1820   French chemists Pierre-Joseph Pelletier and Joseph Bien-aimé Caventou isolate compounds in cinchona bark, creating the first standard dosage of quinine to treat malaria.

1861–1865   Malaria kills at least ten thousand soldiers fighting in the American Civil War.

1874   DDT is first synthesized by German University of Strasbourg doctoral student Othmar Zeidler, but the chemical's insecticidal properties are not discovered until the 1930s.

1880   French physician Charles-Louis-Alphonse Laveran first views the malaria parasite under a microscope.

1880s   The Dutch establish cinchona plantations on Java in Indonesia and quickly develop a global monopoly on quinine.

1890s   British army physician Ronald Ross builds on the work of Laveran by attempting to trace the life cycle of the malaria parasite. Ross's work leads to the discovery by Italian scientist Giovanni Batista Grassi in 1898 that mosquitoes are the disease vector, or carrier.

1905–1910   The building of the Panama Canal is hampered by waves of severe malaria infection among workers.

1914   At least six hundred thousand cases of malaria are reported in the United States. Leaders of the U.S. Public Health Service approach Congress for funding to combat malaria across the country and around southern military bases in particular.

1914–1918   Malaria has a devastating effect on Allied forces fighting in World War I. Approximately 80 percent of French troops fighting in Macedonia contract the disease.

1933   The administration of U.S. president Franklin Delano Roosevelt responds to the Great Depression and the recurring threat of malaria across the country by instituting the Tennessee Valley Authority (TVA). The TVA is charged with harnessing the Tennessee River for hydroelectric power and developing the region's waterways, but it also creates a massive malaria control program that provides both insecticides and window screens for residents. By 1947 malaria is largely controlled in the southern United States.

1939   Swiss scientist Paul Hermann Müller discovers that DDT is highly effective as an insecticide. Müller wins the 1948 Nobel Prize in Physiology or Medicine for his work.

1942   Japanese forces advance in the Dutch East Indies during World War II, overtaking the island of Java and cutting off the world supply of quinine. About sixty thousand U.S. troops die of malaria in the South Pacific and Africa during the war. As a result, dependence on quinine as the sole treatment for malaria is abandoned, and researchers begin experimenting with synthetic alternatives. Allied forces mount an aerial spraying campaign of DDT over the South Pacific.

1946   The United States Communicable Disease Center is created. Later known as the Centers for Disease Control and Prevention, the group's focus is on eradicating malaria in the country, which it succeeds in doing by 1951.

1955   The World Health Organization begins a global eradication campaign that includes indoor and outdoor insecticide spraying, the use of antimalarial drugs, and surveillance of endemic areas. The Indian subcontinent experiences a substantial drop in the number of malaria cases, but other target regions have less success. The campaign encounters drug and insecticide resistance, lack of funding, and political turmoil in endemic countries and is abandoned in 1972.

1960s   The Chinese military begins testing alternatives to quinine and chloroquine, to which falciparum malaria is showing resistance. In 1972 they isolate artemisinin in the leaves of the Artemisia plant. The drug is found to be the most effective treatment for malaria in history.

1962   Rachel Carson's *Silent Spring* is published. The book indicts pesticides, particularly DDT, for their role in the destruction of natural habitats, apparent poisoning of bird and fish populations, and carcinogenic effects on humans and launches the environmental movement. DDT becomes a point of contention between environmentalists and antimalaria activists.

1972   DDT is banned in the United States.

1980s   The World Health Organization begins to research the effectiveness of insecticide-treated bed nets in preventing the spread of malaria.

1987   Colombian biochemist Manuel Elkin Patarroyo develops the first synthetic vaccine against malaria. Although it shows promise, it does not succeed in clinical trials.

2000 The United Nations ratifies its Millennium Development Goals, which include the eradication of malaria by 2015.

2004 The Stockholm Convention on Persistent Organic Pollutants is ratified by 151 signatory countries, instituting a global ban on nine out of twelve dangerous chemical pesticides and limiting the use of DDT to malaria control.

2005 High-profile bed net campaigns gain public interest, resulting in the distribution of millions of nets a year in sub-Saharan African countries by nonprofit groups.

2007 The Bill & Melinda Gates Foundation commits $1 billion to fight malaria and partners with the PATH Malaria Vaccine Initiative to develop a viable vaccine.

2009 Clinical trials of Maryland-based biomedical company Sanaria's malaria vaccine are set to begin on adult volunteers at the U.S. Naval Medical Research Clinical Trials Center in Bethesda and the Center for Vaccine Development at the University of Maryland School of Medicine in Baltimore.

ORGANIZATIONS TO CONTACT

The editors have compiled the following list of organizations concerned with the issues debated in this book. The descriptions are derived from materials provided by the organizations. All have publications or information available for interested readers. The list was compiled on the date of publication of the present volume; the information provided here may change. Be aware that many organizations take several weeks or longer to respond to inquiries, so allow as much time as possible.

African Malaria Network Trust (AMANET)
302 Ring St., off Rose Garden Rd.
Mikocheni A
PO Box 33207
Dar es Salaam
Tanzania
+255 22 2700018
fax: +255 22 2700380
www.amanet-trust.org

AMANET is an Africa-wide program that was originally implemented to promote research and development of a malaria vaccine. It has since evolved to include support for widespread malaria prevention and treatment. The group publishes an annual report and a twice-yearly newsletter.

Bill & Melinda Gates Foundation
PO Box 23350
Seattle, WA 98102
(206) 709-3100
www.gatesfoundation
.org

The Bill & Melinda Gates Foundation has a special interest in reducing global malaria through developing improved antimalarial medications, malaria prevention techniques, expanded funding for malaria control, and vaccine research. The Gates Foundation partners with the PATH Malaria Vaccine Initiative, the Roll Back Malaria Partnership, and the Global Fund to Fight AIDS, Tuberculosis, and Malaria.

Centers for Disease Control and Prevention (CDC)
1600 Clifton Rd.
Atlanta, GA 30333
800-CDC-INFO
(800-232-4636)
TTY: 888-232-6348
www.cdc.gov

The CDC is a public health agency run by the Department of Health and Human Services and is the primary U.S.-based source of information on health and diseases both in the United States and abroad. Fact sheets on malaria and links to resources and articles such as "Preventing Malaria in Travelers" are all available through its Web site.

The Global Fund to Fight AIDS, Tuberculosis, and Malaria
Geneva Secretariat
Chemin de
Blandonnet 8
1214 Vernier
Geneva, Switzerland
+41 58 791 1700
fax: +41 58 791 17 01
www.theglobalfund.org

The Global Fund is a partnership among multiple public and private sector governments, communities, and organizations to fund treatment and prevention of AIDS, tuberculosis, and malaria in 140 countries. The fund publishes an annual report and a newsletter.

Malaria Foundation International
2120 Spencers Way
Stone Mountain, GA
30087
www.malaria.org

The Malaria Foundation International is a U.S.-based nonprofit organization that works in conjunction with other groups to disseminate information on the disease and develop antimalaria projects in endemic countries.

Malaria No More
432 Park Ave. South
13th Fl.
New York, NY 10016
(212) 792-7929
www.malarianomore
.org

Malaria No More is a nongovernmental organization determined to end malaria deaths. It acts as a catalyst to maximize opportunities to save lives through communications, resources, and investments.

Nothing But Nets
United Nations
Foundation
PO Box 96539
Washington, DC
20090-6539
www.nothingbutnets
.net

Nothing But Nets is a nonprofit organization that was created as a result of a column written by sports journalist Rick Reilly about malaria in *Sports Illustrated* with the cooperation of the United Nations Foundation. Its purpose is to enlist the public to donate money to purchase and distribute insecticide-treated bed nets.

PATH Malaria Vaccine Initiative
7500 Old Georgetown
Rd.
Ste. 1200
Bethesda, MD 20814
www.malariavaccine
.org

PATH Malaria Vaccine Initiative is an international vaccine research group funded by a grant from the Bill & Melinda Gates Foundation with the mandate of accelerating the development of a malaria vaccine. It publishes numerous reports on its progress in research and development, clinical trials, and vaccine technology.

President's Malaria Initiative (PMI)
USAID/Ronald Reagan Bldg.
1300 Pennsylvania Ave. NW
Washington, DC 20523
(202) 712-0627
www.fightingmalaria .gov

PMI is an interagency effort by the U.S. government, which includes the U.S. Agency for International Development (USAID) and the Centers for Disease Control and Prevention (CDC), to increase support for malaria initiatives in endemic countries. PMI publishes an annual report and strategic plan.

Roll Back Malaria (RBM) Partnership
World Health Organization
20 Avenue Appia
1211 Geneva 27
Switzerland
+41 22 791 5869
fax: +41 22 791 1587
www.rollbackmalaria .org

The RBM Partnership was formed in 1998 by the World Health Organization, UNICEF, the United Nations Development Program, and the World Bank to coordinate global malaria eradication efforts. It publishes a *Global Malaria Action Plan* as well as other resources about the disease.

World Health Organization (WHO)
20 Avenue Appia
1211 Geneva 27
Switzerland
+ 41 22 791 2111
fax: +41 22 791 3111

The health agency of the United Nations, WHO provides leadership on global health matters. The organization publishes information on malaria for travelers, fact sheets, and an annual *World Malaria Report*. It also hosts an annual World Malaria Day to commemorate the global effort to eradicate the disease.

FOR FURTHER READING

Books

Mark Honigsbaum, *The Fever Trail: Malaria, the Mosquito, and the Quest for Quinine.* London: Pan, 2002.

Margaret Humphreys, *Malaria: Poverty, Race, and Public Health in the United States.* Baltimore: Johns Hopkins University Press, 2001.

Randall M. Packard, *The Making of a Tropical Disease: A Short History of Malaria.* Baltimore: Johns Hopkins University Press, 2007.

Fiametta Rocco, *The Miraculous Fever-Tree: Malaria and the Quest for a Cure That Changed the World.* New York: Harper-Collins, 2003.

Robert Sallares, *Malaria and Rome: A History of Malaria in Ancient Italy.* New York: Oxford University Press, 2002.

Richard Tren, Roger Bate, and Harold M. Koenig, *Malaria and the DDT Story.* London: Institute of Economic Affairs, 2001.

James L.A. Webb Jr., *Humanity's Burden: A Global History of Malaria.* Cambridge, UK: Cambridge University Press, 2008.

Periodicals

Eliza Barclay, "Charity vs. Capitalism in Africa," *Business Week,* January 2, 2008.

Roger Bate, "China's Bad Medicine: The Counterfeit Drug Trade Is a Problem Beijing Can Cure," *Wall Street Journal Asia,* May 5, 2009.

Laura Blue, "Global Malaria Estimates Are Reduced," *Time,* September 18, 2008.

Mary Carmichael and Jaime Cunningham, "On the Trail of a Ferocious Killer," *Newsweek,* October 6, 2008.

Andy Coghlan, "Malaria Vaccine Halves Infections in Trials," *New Scientist,* December 8, 2008.

Thomas Fuller, "Spread of Malaria Feared as Drug Loses Potency," *New York Times,* January 26, 2009.

Reuben Kyama and Donald G. McNeil Jr., "Distribution of Nets Splits Malaria Fighters," *New York Times*, October 9, 2007.

Kim Larsen, "Bad Blood," *OnEarth: An Independent Publication of the Natural Resources Defense Council*, Winter 2008.

Edith Lederer, "UN Says Money Available for Antimalaria Bed Nets," *Washington Post*, April 24, 2009.

Los Angeles Times, "Net Gains for Africa," August 7, 2005.

Donald G. McNeil Jr., "Eradicate Malaria? Doubters Fuel Debate," *New York Times*, March 4, 2008.

———, "Subsidy Plan Seeks to Cut Malaria Drug Cost," *New York Times*, April 17, 2009.

Catharine Paddock, "Antimalaria Gene Confers Higher HIV Risk in People of African Descent," *Medical News Today*, July 17, 2008.

Science Daily, "Can We Restore Wetlands and Leave the Mosquitoes Out?" May 27, 2004.

Christopher Shea, "A Handout, Not a Hand Up: A Popular Approach to 'Sustainable Development' Doesn't Work, Critics Say," *Boston Globe*, November 11, 2007.

Washington Post, "A-Twitter About Malaria: An Unusual Competition Brings Attention to a Killer Disease," April 25, 2009.

Internet Sources

Eliza Barclay, "Climate Change Fueling Malaria in Kenya, Experts Say," January 9, 2008. www.nationalgeographicnews.com/news.

e! Science News, "Most Detailed Malaria Map Ever Highlights Hope and Challenges Facing Global Community," March 24, 2009. www.esciencenews.com/articles/2009/03/24/most.de tailed.malaria.map.ever.highlights.hope.and.challenges.facing .global.community.

IRIN: Humanitarian News and Analysis, "Killer Number One: The Fight Against Malaria," January 2006. www.irinnews.org/InDepthMain.aspx?InDepthID=10&ReportId=57920.

Darren Osborne, "Scientists Map More Malaria Strains," *ABC Science*, October 9, 2008. www.abc.net.au/science/articles/2008/10/09/2386395.htm.

Joanne Silberner, "WHO Backs Use of DDT Against Malaria," *All Things Considered*, National Public Radio, September 15, 2006. www.npr.org.

INDEX

A

Aciro, Santina, 101, 103
Acridine orange, 21
ACT (artemisinin-based combination therapy) treatment, 127, 128, 130
Aedes mosquitoes, 83
Africa
    DDT to control malaria in, 48–53
    malaria epidemics in, *84,* 122–126
    See also specific countries
Agency for Toxic Substances and Disease Registry (ATSDR), 62
Alexander the Great, 28–29
Amollo, Stella, 104
Anemia, 119
Anopheles mosquitoes, *15,* 83, 125
Artemisinin, 23
    source of, 106
    See also ACT treatment
Asian tiger mosquito, *95*
Attaran, Amir, 57
Azithromycin, 17

B

Bed nets. *See* Insecticide-treated nets
Bill & Melinda Gates Foundation, 37, 44, 46
Borneo (Indonesia), 10–12
Breeding Bird Survey, 60

Buj, Valentina, 63
Bush, George W, *40, 50*
    antimalaria funding pledged by, 27
    malaria initiative of, 49

C

Camillus, Katie, 100
Cancer, 62
Carson, Rachel, 12, 33, 49, 51, *58,* 60
Cecilia, Amal, 104–106
Centers for Disease Control and Prevention (CDC), 55
Chavasse, Desmond, 81
Chikungunya fever, 94, 95
Children
    diarrhea as killer of, 85–86
    in Mali, 128
    malaria and, *32*
Chinese goldenthread *(Coptis chinensis),* 23
Chloroquine (Cleocin), 23
    falciparum malaria resistant to, 22
    introduction of, 30
    resistance to, 33
Climate change/global warming
    malaria and, 82–86, 93–98
Clindamycin (Cleocin), 22

Curtis, Chris, 66

D
Day, Karen, 13
DDT (dichloro-diphenyl-
trichloroethane)
African countries must have access to,
48–53
ban on, 33, 51
to control malaria, *11*, 54, 59–65
discovery of, 10, 31
early warnings about, 57
mosquito resistance to, 34, 64
toxicity of, 12
Deaths
from malaria, 17, 63, 110
of newborns due to malaria in
pregnancy, 37
from vector-borne diseases, 86
DEET (insect repellent), 24–25
Deforestation, *91*, 92
increases rate of malaria, *97*
Dengue fever, 83–84, 95
Diagnosis, 38
Diarrhea, 94
as killer of children, 85–86
Dihydroartemisinin, 17
Disease vectors, 83
Dlugash, Mark, 100
Drug resistance
of falciparum malaria, 22–23
of malaria parasites, 33–34

E
El Niño, 94

Ellis, Amy, 117
Environmental Protection Agency
(EPA), 62
Ethiopia, 72

F
Financial Times (newspaper), 57
Finkel, Michael, 26
Fry, Michael, 61, 64
Fumigation, *85*

G
Gates, Bill, 27, 108–116, *111*
Gates, Melinda, *111*
Genomics of *Plasmodium* species,
13–14
Global Malaria Eradication
Programme (World Health
Organization), 31–33
Goldenseal *(Hydrastis canadensis)*, 23
Grant, Ulysses S., 29
Guillet, Pierre, 64
Gwadz, Robert, 28

H
Halofantrine, 23
Helen, Akello, 106
Helm, Kristi, 108
Herbal treatments, 23
Hesse, Gerhard, 57
Histadine-rich protein II (HRP2), 21
HIV infection
gender inequality and, 41
malaria in pregnancy and, 37–38
malaria infection and, 70

I

India, 96

Indoor residual spraying (IRS), 11

Insecticide-treated nets (ITNs), *68*

  African children and, 114

  cost of, 102

  distribution in seven African
    countries, 71, *73*

  distribution should be subsidized,
    77–81

  should be distributed for free, 66–75

Integrated vector management, 65

Intergovernmental Panel on Climate
  Change (IPCC), 89, 90–91

Intermittent preventive treatment
  (IPT), 39

K

Kent, Rebekah, 122

Kochi, Arata, 63

L

Lancet (journal), 97

Lincoln, Abraham, 29

Long-lasting insecticidal bednets
  (LLINs). *See* Insecticide-treated nets

M

Making Pregnancy Safer program
  (WHO), 39

Malaria

  cerebral, 124

  children and, *32*

  cycle of, *19*

  DDT cannot eradicate, 54

  DDT to control, 48–53

  eradication of, 108–116

  falciparum, 20–21, 22–23

  gender and, 41

  in human history, 28–29

  modern medicine and, 127–131

  mothers and, 117–121

  number of people infected annually,
    114

  percent of cases due to *Plasmodium*
    species, 13

  during pregnancy, 24, 36–41, *38*

  symptoms of, 20

  transmission of, 18–20, 124–125

  in Vietnam, 29, *52*

Malawi, 79–81

Mali, 128

Medications to prevent malaria, 30

  advice for travelers on, 25

  falciparum malaria resistant to, 22–23

  malaria parasites resistant to, 33–34

  and the poor, 77–81

Mefloquin (Lariam), 22

Microglossa pyrifolia, 23

Milk thistle (*Silybum marianum*), 23

Millennium Development Goals, 115

Miller, Louis, 34

Mosquitoes, *15, 95*

  as malaria control strategy, 24

  in malaria infection cycle, *19*

  oocyst in stomach wall of, *125*

  resistance to DDT in, 57, 64

  resistance to pesticides in California, *56*

  transmission of malaria by, 18–20,
    124–125

Müller, Paul Hermann, 10, 31

N
National Institutes of Health (NIH), 114
Neira, Maria, 63
New Deal, 55
New England Journal of Medicine, 43, 97
New York Times (newspaper), 55

O
Operation Cat Drop, 12, 13
Osterholm, Michael, 96–97

P
Pesticides, 56
Plasmodium falciparum, 13, 18, 18
  difficulty in developing vaccine against, 34–35
  malaria caused by, 20–21
Plasmodium malariae, 16
Plasmodium ovale, 16, 23
Plasmodium vivax, 16, 20, 23
Poverty
  malaria and, 57–58
  sick children and, 100–107
Pregnancy, 21, 38
Prevention efforts, 24
  costs of interventions in sub-Saharan Africa, 90
  mosquitoes and, 24
  for pregnant women, 39
  in Vietnam, 52
Primaquine, 23

Public Health Service, U.S., 55

Q
Quarterly News of the Association of Former WHO Staff (newsletter), 12
Quinine
  discovery of, 29
  drawbacks of, 30
  production of from cinchona tree, 2, 30
  source of, 106

R
Rabinovich, Regina, 113
Reiter, Peter, 87
Robbins, Chandler, 60–61
Roberts, Donald, 62
Roosevelt, Franklin D., 55
Rosenberg, Tina, 55
Ross, Ronald, 13, 14
Rwanda, malaria cases in, 78

S
Sachs, Jeffrey D., 66
Santina, Aciro, 101, 103
Schwartz, Peter, 98
Screens, window, 10
Shah, Sonia, 54
Siad, Maria, 93
Silent Spring (Carson), 12, 33, 49, 51, 60
Solomon, Gina, 98
Stéphenne, Jean, 42
Stockholm Convention in Persistent Organic Pollutants, 62, 63–64
Sulfadoxone/pyrimethamine (Fansidar), 22

T
Teklehaimanot, Awash, 66
Tennessee Valley Authority, 55
Thuma, Phil, 126
Treatment(s), 22–23
  alternative, 23
  costs of interventions in sub-Sahara
    Africa, *90*
  of falciparum malaria, 22–23
  in Uganda, 103
  See also Medications to prevent malaria
Turkington, Carol A., 16

U
Uganda
  malaria prevention/treatment in,
    101–107
  sources of antimalarial drugs in, *105*
  tests use of insecticide Icon, 49–51
UNICEF (United Nations Children's
  Fund), 77, 80
United States
  eradication of malaria in, 10, 109
  malaria as growing problem in, 17

V
Vaccine, malaria
  challenges in developing, 24

estimated funds needed for, *61*
  existing vaccines *vs.*, 45
RTSS
  effectiveness of, *46*
  shows promise, 42–46
Vietnam
  malaria among U.S. troops in, 29
  prevention efforts in, *52*
Voices for a Malaria-Free Future,
  127

W
Washington, George, 29
Women, 36–41
Women Deliver, 36
World Health Organization
  (WHO), 10, 82, 114
  DDT use recommended by, 51
  launches malaria eradication
    program, 31
  mosquito control efforts of, 24
  preventive efforts aimed at
    pregnant women, 39–40
Wormwood *(Artemesia annua)*, 23

Z
Zambia, 122–126
Zaramba, Sam, 48